WITHIN HOSPITAL WALLS:

AN INSIDE LOOK AT CHEMICAL DEPENDENCY TREATMENT

KATHRYN KORNEGAY, PhD, RN

A Nurse Owned Company

VISTA PUBLISHING, INC.

Edited by Carolyn S. Zagury, MS, RN, CPC

Cover design by Thomas Taylor of Thomcatt Graphics

Vista Publishing, Inc.
473 Broadway
Long Branch, NJ 07740
(908) 229-6500

Printed and bound in the United States of America

First Edition

ISBN: 1-880254-31-X

Library of Congress Catalog Care Number: 95-61473

U.S.A. Price $14.95
Canada Price $19.95

DEDICATION

This book is dedicated to those who are still suffering and to those who are seeking and supporting a recovery pathway.

MEET THE AUTHOR

Kathryn Kornegay has worked in the field of psychiatric and chemical dependency nursing for over twenty-five years. She has taught psychiatric nursing at the University of Kansas School of Nursing, at the University of Texas Health Science Center, San Antonio, and at Southeast Missouri State University. She has been an active advocate for developing peer assistance programs for nurses and student nurses. Dr. Kornegay has acted as a consultant to the Texas Peer Assistance Program for Nurses and to a variety of psychiatric and chemical dependency facilities. She is certified as a Chemical Dependency Nurse Specialists.

Dr. Kornegay's work with students and her research addressing chemical dependency and recovery as experienced by chemically dependent nurses has been published in a variety of national journals. The majority of her work has been published under her previous name of Dr. Kathryn Sisney.

Personally, Dr. Kornegay has enjoyed over fourteen years of recovery from chemical dependency. She recently married a man who has over twenty-three years of recovery, and their recovery pathway has carried them to the Ozark foothills where they are enjoying the challenges and serenity of isolated rural life. Dr. Kornegay is currently an Associate Professor at Southeast Missouri State University in Cape Girardeau, Missouri. She welcomes your input and she may be reached at the following address and phone number:

Southeast Missouri State University
One University Plaza
Cape Girardeau, MO 63701
(314) 651-2855.

PREFACE

Within Hospital Walls provides the reader with an inside look at chemical dependency health care from the perspective of both the clients it serves and those who work in the field. Its short stories allow the reader to vicariously experience a variety of scenarios associated with chemical dependence and its recovery. In addition, they allow the reader to learn about a variety of topics such as withdrawal, gender bias, relapse, defusing staff conflict, and working a twelve step program. The author's use of story telling effortlessly teaches about such complex concepts and overtly challenges culturally biased attitudes.

The short stories are based on the author's more than twenty-five years of working in the field as well as her over fourteen years of personal recovery. This rich experiential background lets her draw on a myriad of stories and experiences to provide the reader with a multi-faceted exposure to the "chemical dependency sub-culture." Consequently, this book is ideal for those new to the health care field of chemical dependency whether they be students or seasoned health care veterans interested in enlarging their scope of expertise. In addition, it is also an excellent introduction to the subject matter for anyone who is interested in learning about chemical dependence and recovery. As such, it will provide insight, empathy, hope and guidance for those who seek it out of personal need or interested curiosity.

The reader interested in specific etiologies or complicated biochemical theories is referred to more traditional textbooks. The aim of ***Within Hospital Walls*** is to elicit emotion, feeling and empathy in the reader. The content is not scientific in its approach. The best way to read this book is with an open mind. Be prepared to enjoy, feel, laugh, cry . . . and learn.

TABLE OF CONTENTS

TABLE OF CONTENTS

UNIT ONE

ENTERING RECOVERY

Chapter I

HITTING HOME

Hilary found herself tossing and turning. She couldn't get back to sleep. Sleep? That was a joke. She'd never been able to get really comfortable since she hit the bed. Her head hurt. It didn't get any better when it suddenly dawned on her that she couldn't remember how she'd got home.

She forced herself to raise up on one elbow and look at the clock. Yikes! She was late to work. Again. As she slowly sat up, she began to try to remember what had happened the night before. She remembered going out with the gang after work for a few drinks. At least that was how it started. She remembered dancing, flirting, having fun. She also remembered getting dizzy and how funny it was when she had trouble talking clearly. She remembered kissing some guy she met, and he'd wanted to take her home. She had been still sober enough to refuse his offer. After that she couldn't remember what happened.

She got out of bed and walked into the bathroom. The first thing she did was drink a glass of water. Then she noticed that the toilet was filthy. She must have thrown up and been so out of it she didn't clean it up before she crawled into bed. She leaned over and closed the lid on the toilet before she headed for her roommate's door. She smelled coffee brewing in the kitchen and headed that way instead.

Her entry into the kitchen was greeted with, "'Bout time you made it up Hilary. You must have really tied one on last night. I had to let you in when you got her this morning. You couldn't even get your key in the door. When you got in you couldn't even talk to me. You were barely able to make it to your bathroom before you threw up. How are you feeling now?"

Hilary grimaced. "Not so good. Would you call my boss and tell her I've got a touch of the flu? Tell her I've been throwing up and I'll try to make it in this afternoon if I feel better." Sally didn't answer, so Hilary poured herself a cup of coffee. She noticed her hand was shaking. She needed to take some aspirin for her headache. They said the 'hair of the dog that bit you' was good for a hangover. Maybe she'd try that. She reached for the coffee liqueur and poured some into her coffee. Glancing up, she noticed Sally frowning at her. "What is it now Sally? Sometimes I'd swear you thought you were my mother instead of my roommate!"

"You know good and well what it is. You're always asking me to call your boss and make excuses for your drinking. When will you start being responsible for yourself so I won't have to act like your mother? Get a grip. You don't have to drink like this. You can have fun after work with friends without drinking. Like they say, 'Just say no.' Sounds simple enough to me."

"Come on Sally, you know I'd call for you if you needed me to call. Besides, you're right. I don't have to drink to have fun. I'll try 'just saying no.' I have as much will power as the next person. You should have seen my father put the stuff away. Compared to him, I'm a civilized social drinker."

"Here we go again. I'm not calling you an alcoholic, Hilary. I'm worried about what you're doing to yourself. You're this close to losing another job. You've had two DUIs in the past six months. Two or three mornings a week you have to have a drink as soon as you get up to get over your hangover. When are you going to realize something's wrong with this picture? I'll call one more time. That's it." Sally turned and walked away. She put on her coat, grabbed her purse and opened the door. Just as she was stepping out onto the porch, Hilary stopped her. "You're sure you'll call as soon as you get to the hospital? Please call before you get wrapped up in morning report. OK? One more thing, do you know how I got home last night?"

Sally frowned. "You have to ask? Look at your car. Two wheels are up on the curb and two are off. Not exactly the kosher way to park. Don't worry. I know how you obsess about these things. I've already checked the car for dents. You were lucky this time. Looks like you made it home without hurting yourself or anyone else."

Hilary closed the door. What was she going to do? Her whole life was a big mess. She was loosing her friends. She was close to losing another job. What scared her the most was she was beginning not to care. All that mattered was drinking. That was the only time she felt good. Suddenly the phone rang. She managed to answer it before the machine did. Then she wished she'd left it for the machine because it was her mother.

"Hilary Sue, where were you last night? It was your sister's birthday, for Christ's sake. You promised to be there for her party. You called and said you were going out with your friends after work. You promised you'd still make it to the party because it didn't start until 8 PM. Do you know how Peggy felt when her only sister didn't even show up? Well, do you?"

"Mom, calm down. Of course I know how she felt. Have you forgotten how many times Dad missed my birthdays? He even missed my graduation. He missed all the things that were important to me. Would I do that to Peggy without a good reason? Of course not!"

"Well, I'm waiting."

"Mom, chill out. I had car trouble. I had to flag down help; I was out in the middle of nowhere, and I couldn't get to a phone. I'm sorry. I'll make it up to her this weekend. Promise."

"You sound more and more like your father every day. I just hope you're not following in his footsteps."

"Mom, what a thing to say! You know I'm not an alcoholic like Dad is."

"OK. Just remember to make it home this weekend. I'll explain to Peggy what happened. If you'd call her this afternoon when she gets home from school, I know It would help her feel better."

"OK Mom. Gotta run. I'm late for work. 'Bye."

"'Bye."

* * * * *

Sally was on her coffee break. She was sitting in the pediatric staff lounge staring out the window. She'd make the call for Hilary. She couldn't stop worrying about her. As far as she could tell, Hilary was exhibiting all the signs of alcoholism .... at least the ones they'd covered in her psychiatric nursing class. Something had to be done, but what?

Her instructor had talked about something called an "intervention." She said a group of concerned people confronted the alcoholic with the consequences of his or her drinking.[1] There was something else, what was it? Oh yea, something about this approach breaking through the alcoholic's denial so the alcoholic would get help for their disease. Would something like this work with Hilary? How would she even begin to get one set up? She sat and stared out the window for a long time. Then she picked up the phone to call Alice. Alice was a friend who worked on the hospital's

---

[1] McElmurry, B.J., Church, O.M., and Haack, M.R. Intervention with nurses in academia and administration. In Haack, M.R. and Hughes, T.L. (Eds.), Addiction in the Nursing Profession. New York: Springer Publishing Company, 1989, pp. 97-112.

chemical dependency unit. She'd know what to do. Sally knew she could trust her to keep all of this confidential.

"Alice, this is Sally. Listen, I've got a problem. I need some help solving this one. Do you think we could get together on our lunch break? There was a brief silence, then Alice responded. "What's going on? You sound upset. Sure we can get together, but I'd like to know what's bothering you first." Sally swallowed hard before replying, "Oh, it's my roommate. I think she has a drinking problem. I want to talk to you about something I remember from nursing school. I think they called it an "intervention." Do you think we could talk about setting one up?"

"Sure," Alice replied. "we'll talk about it. I'm sorry it's come to this. Try not to worry about it. Together we'll come up with something. How about meeting me in the dining room about 1:00 PM? It shouldn't be crowded then and we can have a semblance of privacy."

What a relief. It sounded like Alice would be lots of help. "Thanks. I'll get my break changed over to then. Let's do it."

* * * * *

Two days later, Hilary's mother, Peggy, Hilary's employer, and Hilary's father met with the clinical nurse specialist (CNS) in her office on the chemical dependence treatment unit. They were there to plan an intervention intended to get Hilary to seek treatment for her alcoholism. Sally contacted the clinical nurse specialist and Hilary's mother. Hilary's mother asked Hilary's employer, her sister and her father to participate in the intervention. Getting them all together had been easier than Sally had anticipated.

The clinical nurse specialist began the session by introducing herself. "Hello. My name is Ms. Tredwell. I'm the clinical nurse specialist on this unit. I'll be helping you confront Hilary in a caring way. It is our hope that she'll decide to do something about her problem. Let's get started by introducing ourselves and telling each other why we are here. I want to remind you that everything said here or during the intervention itself is to be kept confidential. OK, let's start with Sally."

"My name's Sally. I've been Hilary's roommate for five years. In the beginning she drank socially just like everyone else. In the past year or so her drinking has been different. She's lost several jobs, had several DUIs, drinks by herself, and drinks early in the morning to combat hangovers. She can't remember things that happen when she's drinking. She's getting harder and harder to live with these days. She's irritable. I think it's because she's feeling guilty and depressed. I'm at my wits end. I'm sorry about her, and I don't know what to do to help her. That's why I started all this, and that's why I called her mother."

The CNS spoke up. "That's a good lead into Hilary's mother. Mrs. Jenkins, would you go next, please?"

Mrs. Jenkins looked uncomfortable. When she did talk, her voice was soft and hard to hear. "I've seen this day coming for a long time. I've done everything humanly possible to keep this from happening. You know how alcoholism runs in families. I married an alcoholic and had his children. So I guess I shouldn't be surprised. I love Hilary. That's why I'm here. My Henry's been sober now for over five years. If we can spare our Hilary a lot of the pain he went through and if we can get her into the kind of recovery he's found, going through this public humiliation will be worth it."

Hilary's father was partically squirming in his chair. As soon as he could, he broke into the conversation. "I want to go next. I don't see this as a public humiliation. I see it as a chance for us to help Hilary. This is all about a disease. It's not a moral question at all. I'm Hilary's father. The alcoholic. The villain in all this, the carrier of the genes. I'm proud to be able to say that I am a recovering alcoholic. I'm here to help my daughter find what I found. If I'm honest, I have to admit I'm hoping helping her this way will help me make up for all the times I let her down while she was growing up."

The CNS smiled at Mr. Jenkins. Then she glanced towards an attractive, well dressed young woman who had a clipboard in her hands. "Thank you Mr. Jenkins. Now, Ms. Jones, would you please introduce yourself."

The young woman set the clipboard down on the side table next to the sofa upon which she was sitting. "I'm Ms. Jones, Ms. Jenkins' employer. I've been her employer for only three months. I don't know her as well as the rest of you do. She has a lot of potential. My company has a very active employee's assistance program that helps our alcoholic employees seek recovery. I checked with our central office about our company's policies before coming today. I got their backing to promise Ms. Jenkins that if she seeks treatment for her alcoholism, she'll have her job waiting for her when she gets out of treatment."

Again, the CNS smiled. "That's good news." Then she turned to the young girl sitting quietly in the corner. "Now, Peggy, it's your turn."

Her voice was soft and serious as she began talking. "I'm Hilary's little sister. I don't really understand what's going on here. I do know Hilary missed my birthday. She called me to apologize. She was crying. Nothing she said made any sense. She just kept saying 'I'm sorry' over and over. It was like she kept forgetting what she was saying. Her words ran together. It was hard to understand what she was saying."

The room was quiet. Then Ms. Tredwell broke the silence. "Thanks, that was a good beginning. Now I want each of you to think about something or several things you have personally observed that indicate Hilary has a problem with drinking. You'll share these and your feeling about them with Hilary. I also want you to think about how you are going to tell Hilary that you love her and are concerned for her. Once we've figured out the specific incidents with which you want to confront her, I'll help each of you write what you are going to say to her about them and your feelings. This will serve as a script for you to follow when we do the actual intervention. Then we'll run through a rehearsal several times. That way it will be easier to do when we do it for real. It's important not to communicate anger or blame during the intervention. We need to focus on your love, your concern, and specific behaviors you've observed. It's also important for her to see and accept she has a problem. She'd probably just get defensive if we told her. If we get caught up in the labels, she could just get angry and stop listening. OK, let's get to work."

* * * * *

On the afternoon of the intervention everyone except Hilary and her mother were sitting in Ms. Tredwell's office. Ms. Jenkins had taken Hilary shopping and out to lunch. It was Hilary's day off. She and Ms. Jenkins made a practice of doing this together from time to time. That was why Hilary hadn't been suspicious when her mother called and asked her to go shopping. On the way back from their shopping trip, Hilary's mother made an unexpected turn into the hospital's parking lot.

Hilary was confused. She turned and looked at her Mom. "Why did you stop here? Have you gone senile on me?"

Ms. Jenkins looked extremely uncomfortable. Her mouth was dry. Finally, she managed to say, "I was afraid to tell you over lunch. You remember me saying Peggy was upset when you missed her birthday? We've been having some problems with her since then. Somehow I think it's related into your missing her party. Anyway, I promised her therapist you and I'd stop by and talk to her about what it was like when you were at home and Peggy was younger. I hope you don't mind. I think it'll help your sister."

Hilary's mouth dropped open. She glared at her mother. "How could you make plans like this without asking me? I feel manipulated. I'll do it, but don't think I'm doing it because of you and your schemes. I'm doing it for Peggy because I know what it's like to grow up in a dysfunctional home."

Now both Hilary and her mother looked hurt. Her mother quietly said, "Let's go in; we're late as it is."

Hilary followed her into the office. As she turned from closing the door she realized there were other people in the office. Of course, Peggy was there. Her father was there too. Why was Sally there? And her boss. What could she possibly have to do with all this? The strange woman who must be the therapist was walking toward her with her hand outstretched. Hilary took it and shook it. She was saying, "Hilary, I'm Ms. Tredwell. I'm a psychiatric clinical nurse specialist. The people in this room asked me to help them talk to you about their concern for you. I need you to agree to listen to what each of them has to say without interrupting. When they have all talked, then it will be your turn to respond. At that time you'll be able to say anything you wish. Agreed?"

Hilary felt dazed. She'd been tricked. This wasn't about Peggy at all. This room was full of people here to gang up on her! Finally, she was able to stammer, "Uh . . . th . . . this is crazy. I, I . . . what's going on here anyway?"

The CNS answered her. "Please, just listen and don't interrupt. It'll all make sense eventually. They want to talk to you. All that's said will be kept confidential. Now, sit down and listen."

Hilary sat down. "OK, OK. I'm warning you, I don't like the way I was tricked into this. If I need to contact my lawyer before this is all over, I promise you I will."

The CNS and everyone else ignored her comment. The CNS turned to Sally and calmly said, "Sally, you start."

Sally swallowed a sip of her soda before she began speaking. "Uh, I can understand you being upset about being tricked into being here. That was the only way we could think of to get you here. I've been worried about you for months now. Your friendship means the whole world to me. I can't just stand by and watch you throw it away. We used to have so much fun. Now all we do is fight. You're always wanting me to call your boss or your family and make excuses for you. You've lost several jobs. You've got a hangover every morning when you get up, and the first thing you do is take a drink so your hands will stop shaking. The worst thing is you don't remember what you did while you're drinking. You don't remember how you get home from the bars and parties. You have to go out every morning and check your car to see if you ran into anything or anyone. That has to be scary for you. You've stopped dating. You stay in your room all the time when you're not out drinking. I find your bottles hidden all over the house. I'm sacred for you, and I want things to get better for you. Please, please look at what you are doing to yourself. There is help. You're not alone in this."

Hilary couldn't believe she was hearing this. "Sally, how could you say those things in front of all these people? I thought you were my friend. Live and learn. Thanks loads. I can't believe you've turned on me like this. I don't have a drinking problem, not a real one. You bitch. For two cents . ."

The CNS interrupted her in mid-sentence. "Hilary, you agreed to stay quiet until everyone was done. You'll get your turn."

Hilary closed her mouth, sighed, shrugged her shoulders, sat back in her chair and glared across the room at Sally. Then she glared at everyone in turn. When her eyes fell on Peggy, she looked away. She couldn't stand to see the hurt in her eyes.

The tense silence was broken by Hilary's Mom. The old busy body couldn't wait to get her two cent's worth in on this one. "Hilary, I saw this happen with your father. I don't want you to have to go through everything he did. You're my oldest daughter. I almost lost you with a miscarriage. I don't want to loose you know. We've come through too much together. You've got an education, lots of potential. You've got your whole life ahead of you. What Sally said is true. You're not alone in this. You have a problem. We want to help you solve it."

Hilary couldn't let her mother finish. She was too angry. "Sure you saw this happen with my father. And you want to know why? Because you were always nagging at him just the way you nag at me."

Once again, the CNS interrupted. "Hilary, you promised. Let your mother finish." Hilary glared at her mother.

Her mother continued. "Last week you missed your sister's ninth birthday party because you were out drinking. You forgot about the party. When you called to apologize, your voice was slurred, and you were crying. You sounded drunk. I was afraid to let you talk to Peggy, but against my better judgment, I did. I decided it was wrong to try to hide the truth from her. And I've decided it's wrong to try to hide the truth from you. Your drinking is causing you and us problems. If you don't do something about it, things will only get worse. You have to face the truth and get help. We're here for you. I'm here for you. I love you. Please listen to us today and love yourself enough to get the help you need."

Her mother was finally done, but for the life of her, Hilary couldn't think of a comeback. Besides, she was supposed to stay quiet. This time she didn't have to be reminded. Her mother sounded genuinely concerned. Maybe things were worse off than she thought. Maybe these people were right. Maybe she did have a drinking problem. Hilary shook her head. She couldn't start thinking like that. Then her father spoke up.

"Hilary what your Mother says is true. We are here for you. I know I wasn't around much when you were young. When I was, I was too drunk to be a good father. I have a chance now to show you how much I love you by helping you see that you are headed the same way. I don't want you to have to experience what I did. I've been sober and in recovery now for almost six years. I've found a way of living that gives me back my self respect and a joy for living. I want that for you. I want you to be able to love yourself and to enjoy your life. You know what a hopeless drunk I was. I've changed; surely you can see that. I have hope in my life now, and I want to share that with you. As sick as I was, if I can find recovery, then I know you can too. Your problem isn't as bad as mine was. I'm trying to spare you that. Please listen with your heart. Give us a chance to help you help yourself."

Hilary rolled her eyes. "Sure, Dad. It's sure easy for you to say that. You're so full of shit. All I ever hear from you these days is all this 'hearts and flowers and ain't recovery beautiful' routine. Get real. Do you really think you can undo the damage you've already done?"

The CNS interrupted before her father could answer. "That's enough Hilary. Your father risked a lot saying what he just said. Remember, listen and don't interrupt. Thanks, Mr. Jenkins. Now Peggy, it's your turn."

Peggy looked at the door like she wished she could escape from this, "let's roast Hilary" party. Then she looked down at the floor. Finally, she looked up and over at Hilary. "I don't really understand what's happened Hilary. You're my only sister. I've always counted on you. You've always been there for me even when mother and daddy weren't. Except lately. You're not there for me. We don't have any fun together anymore. We never go to the movies anymore. We never go skating anymore. We never do anything together anymore. You forgot to show up. Then you call or come by and say you're sorry. You always promise it won't happen again. Then it does. I'm scared Hilary. Real scared. It feels like I've lost a sister and a best friend. I'm worried that it's my fault. Please don't keep hurting yourself. I hate it when you cry. I know you're hurting. I'm sorry. I'm sorry if I've done anything to cause all this. Can things just go back to the way they used to be? I love you. I miss you." Peggy reached for the tissue the CNS was reaching over to her. She wiped at the silent tears glistening on her cheeks.

Hilary couldn't help it. She had tears sliding down her face too. She reached for a tissue. She wanted to wipe them away before anyone saw them. As she reached for it, Sally reached over and grabbed her hand and reassuringly held it. Hilary smiled through her tears. Sally was a good friend after all. Hilary was confused and scared. She was trying to blink away her tears. She was trying to focus on her boss who was talking now.

She was saying, "We've known for some time now at work that you have a problem. We also know that you have lots of potential. The company doesn't want to loose you. We are prepared to hold your job for you. If you seek treatment, it'll be there waiting for you when you get out. If you don't seek treatment, then we'll be forced to terminate your position. We don't want to do that. We do want to support your recovery in any way we can."

Hilary was quiet. Her boss had spoken matter-of-factly. She sounded like she meant what she was saying. Hilary reached for another tissue. To her surprise, the CNS was looking at her. Then she said, "It's your turn to talk now Hilary. We'll all listen."

For once, Hilary was at a loss for words. That usually meant it was time to be honest. "I don't know what to say. I was angry when you guys tricked me and when this exchange started. Part of me is still pissed. I just don't like being ganged up on like this. I'm not an alcoholic like Dad was. I just have trouble once in a while getting home from bars. I heard what you said about me forgetting things. You're right. That scares me a lot. And Peggy, I'm sorry I've not been there for you. I want to be. I don't know what to do. I'm so confused."

The CNS smiled at her and glanced at Peggy, before turning back to say, "Why don't you let Peggy tell you what she'd like you to do?"

Peggy was looking at Hilary with a hopeful expression on her face. "Please, Hilary. For my sake, please go into treatment. You don't have to get hung up on the label 'alcoholic.' That doesn't matter, you do. They'll help you know what to do for your problem so you don't ever have to be like Daddy used to be. They'll help with the forgetting. You won't have to be scared anymore. We can be sisters again. Please."

Hilary smiled at Peggy. Then she looked thoughtfully out the window. She looked down at her hands, They were methodically shredding her damp tissue. She sighed and looked up. No longer able to hide her tears, and glad for Sally's arm around her shoulder, she simply said, "OK."

Chapter II

A NO YAWN NIGHT

Sara caught herself yawning as she reached for her cup of coffee. This evening's shift had been slow. They said that usually meant something was about to happen. You never know in this business. What could it be this time? She reviewed in her mind some of the emergencies that could happen. Her friends who worked the ER told her that she could always expect to see an esophageal bleed someday since she was working with alcoholics. In school they'd taught them that alcoholism affects all of the body's systems.[1] She'd been here two weeks, and all she'd seen that was even close to an emergency was when a hypoglycemic's blood sugar ran low one evening.

Her thoughts were interrupted by Joe coming into the lounge. He'd worked here for years, and he didn't seem to mind working with a new graduate. She'd heard him brag that he'd broken in quite a few. He liked to brag about the old days when they'd called him an orderly. He said they routinely shot up every alcoholic who walked in the door with 100 mg. of Librium to prevent delirium tremens from happening. Everybody got the shots regardless of whether they showed signs of pending withdrawal.

He was heading her way, so she greeted him with, "Hi, Joe. What's happening?"

He matter-of-factly answered, "Not much, Carter's being discharged tomorrow, so I've been helping him get his things together. I've also been pushing the idea of him attending Alcoholics Anonymous (A.A.) after he's out of here. He's still not quite convinced that AA's for him."

She looked up at him and asked, "Is it always this slow?"

He answered, "No. But that doesn't mean something might not happen."

She looked puzzled as she asked, "What could happen? Nothing was mentioned in report. Nobody was admitted today."

---

[1] Hutchinson, S.A. Applying the Nursing Process for clients with Psychoactive Substance Use Disorders. In Wilson H. and Kneisl, C.'s (1988) Psychiatric Nursing. Third Edition, Addison-Wesley Publishing Company, Menlo Park, California, pp. 348-395.

He detected a wistfulness in her comments. He smiled down at her as he replied. "Do I detect a tinge of regret that you decided to try out this specially instead of going for the big bucks on some intensive care unit?"

She laughed, "No, but I'm afraid I'll lose the skills I've learned if I don't get to use them."

He'd heard that one before. "Don't worry about that. You'll have plenty of chances. Let' look back at today's report. Did you notice who'd been here over a day or so?"

Sara frowned. "No, why would I bother doing that?"

Joe sighed. He sounded exasperated as he replied. "They just don't teach you anything in those degree schools do they?"

Sara's frown deepened. "Joe ......"

He responded, "OK, OK. Someone's who has been off their booze for a few hours gets anxious, shaky. Then in one to two days the patient may start hallucinating,[2] and eventually, if untreated, they may experience seizures. Wilson and Kneisel[3] say that withdrawal can start up to 4 days after the person stops drinking. Have you ever seen a full blown case of the DT's?"

She answered, "No, but I know it stands for delirium tremens."

Joe continued, "It's no fun to see. First the patient gets restless and agitated. Then they start hallucinating. They pick at things that aren't there. They can't think straight.[4] They're miserable. And they can die."

Sara was thoughtful as she answered, "I remember my teacher talking about DTs. I never worried about them because she said you could predict them happening by taking the patient's vital signs. If they became elevated, then you sedated them and prevented DTs from happening."

Joe replied, "For the most part, she was right. The sedation thing is tricky. What sedates one person doesn't always sedate another person because they have developed tolerance. I remember this old guy who always used to come in drunk 1-2 days after we discharged him. He invented the revolving door. At that time I was working in a state hospital. He'd come in smelling of alcohol, and we'd give him Librium 100 mg. before we did anything else. It didn't make any difference. He'd always go into a full blown seizure within an hour or two. I guess what I'm trying to tell you is you can't

---

[2] Ray, O. (1983). Drugs, Society & Human Behavior. C.V. Mosby: St. Louis, MO.

[3] Hutchinson, S.A. Applying the Nursing Process for clients with Psychoactive Substance Use Disorders. In Wilson H. and Kneisl, C.'s (1988) Psychiatric Nursing. Third Edition, Addison-Wesley Publishing Company, Menlo Park, California, pp. 348-395.

[4] Ibid.

always count on chemistry saving the day. You have to stay on your toes. In this business, withdrawal is a fact of life, and DTs are too."

When Sara came to work the next day, she was surprised to hear in report that Billings had developed withdrawal during the night. He'd had a seizure, and he was now experiencing DTs. She was assigned to cover him. He was under doctor's orders for sedation and constant observation. That meant she'd be sitting at his bedside all day. Guess Joe had been right. Now maybe she'd learn something about this mysterious malady.

* * * * *

You could here Billings clear out in the hallway. He kept saying: "Gotta get up. Mama needs me. Gotta get up. Let me up."

He was tossing and turning. His face was wet with sweat, and his hair was damp. He kept picking at his pajamas as if there was something on them. Sometimes he'd look at the ceiling and react as if there was something there that scared him.

"Benny, you've got to let me up man. Let's do another round. I'm buying this time."

Billings was fighting the soft waist restraint they had around him. He needed to be kept in bed because he was unsteady on his feet. Besides, he might have another seizure. The side rails were also raised, but they were padded because he might bump them if he had a seizure. He kept trying to get out of bed anyway. Joe had stopped by earlier.

He'd said, "When you let Billings up so he can go to the bathroom, he lets you help him walk the first few steps. Then he gets belligerent and tries to fight you off. So it's better to keep him restrained with the waist posey, get help, and offer him the bedpan or urinal every hour or so."

This time she was ready to listen to Joe.

That reminded her. It was time to offer Billings the urinal again. She spoke up and asked, "Mr. Billings, do you need the urinal?"

Mr. Billings glared at her. "Who the hell are you lady? I don't need some strange broad offerin' to help me pee!" Sara sighed. They'd been through this routine several times now. Billing's memory was effected by the DTs, so he didn't recognize her or remember her even though she had repeatedly introduced herself.

She went through the routine again. "I'm Sara. I'm your nurse this evening. I offered you the urinal because I thought you might need to go to the bathroom."

This time a sly smile crossed Mr. Billings face. "That's all right little darlin'. I'll tell you what you can do for me. Why don't you scoot your pretty little behind into this here bed right next to mine. We could have a lot of fun."

Billings' face contorted. He was momentarily quiet, and then he started mumbling again. Sara was barely able to make out what he was saying.

"Benny, you can't stop now. I'm winning. You can't quit when I'm winning. Come on. Ante up!"

He continued to toss and turn for a few minutes, then he was quiet. He appeared to have drifted off to sleep.

They'd told her there'd be days like this. She was beginning to believe them. They warned her in report that he might have another seizure, so she reviewed in her mind what she should do if he did. She'd need to note what time it started, what time it ended and what type of muscular movements he demonstrated. She'd have to call for help so they'd get the doctor to come administer the IV valium he'd ordered for Mr. Billings if he started having another seizure. They'd bring the suction machine. He might be incontinent of stool or urine, so she would need to clean him up after the seizure ended. He night break the restraint. He'd probably bump the padded side rails repeatedly during the seizure. A patent airway was the most important thing. She remembered that much from school. And if he had a seizure while he was out of bed, she would need to cushion his head from hitting the floor.

She knew he'd eventually be past this part of his withdrawal, but right now it seemed to be lasting an eternity. He was in so much discomfort, and there wasn't much she could do for him. She just had to sit and watch and listen. Sometimes it was hard not to get offended by his hostile or sexual comments. She kept telling herself it was just part of his delirium. She had to keep a vigilant watch over him because he might have another seizure. The medication nurse was seeing that he got sedated around the clock as ordered, but Joe was right. Sometimes that wasn't enough. It sure didn't look like she was going to be yawning tonight!

UNIT TWO

TREATMENT ISSUES

Chapter III

COURAGE

Brad couldn't believe he was having to sit through another meeting like this one. All this "Higher Power" shit. How could these clowns fall for all this powerlessness crap? The only way he could get through these meetings was to tell himself he was researching another paper. Maybe there was enough here for a book. If it hadn't been for his professor threatening to report him to the dean if he didn't seek treatment, he wouldn't be in this mess. But he had, so here he was spending the first summer session as a patient rather than a student. As it was, he was being given an incomplete for last semester's psych class because the professor said he had to do this treatment thing before he'd give him a grade. Shit happens. So they say.

He was jarred out of his thoughts by the counselor asking him for his opinion. He had no idea what the group had been talking about; but he'd be damned if he was going to let this bozo know he hadn't been paying attention. He'd try one of those proverbial "open-ended questions" his professors were always telling him to use with his patients.

He shot his best condescending glance towards the counselor as he said, "My opinion?"

The counselor wasn't fooled by his theatrics. "Very good, Brad. You just used reflection correctly. Now, how about getting out of the role of therapist and into the role of patient. Think you can manage that?"

Brad growled, "Why should I?" He shifted his weight from one hip to another. These chairs got hard. Then he glared at the counselor. Of course he had the nerve to smile back at him. The grin reminded Brad of one cartoonists painted on cat's faces just before the cats pounced on a mouse.

"Now Brad. We all know a 'why question' implies blame. Didn't they teach you better than that in your psychology classes?"

That's it. I'm outta here Brad thought as he stood up to leave the room. He turned to face the counselor and stopped mid-stride. As he spoke, he realized his voice was cracking.

"Lay off me! What gives you the right to be on my case all the time? Just because I'm in graduate school working on becoming a psychologist you think you can pick on me about it all the time. What's the matter? Are you afraid I have more education than you?"

"No. That's not it at all. Sometimes I have to make you angry to get under that tough skin of yours. You've been here a week now, and you haven't really participated in anything yet. Unless you acknowledge that you have a problem and start working on it while you're here, you'll have wasted your time, our time and lots of your insurance company's money."

Brad was aware that he was speaking loudly. His anger was really seeping through. He didn't care. He'd had enough of this bozo being on his case. He grabbed the group room's door knob and turned again towards the counselor. This time he spoke through clenched teeth.

"Problem? Me have a problem? You've got to be kidding! These people have lost jobs, families, fortunes. Some have spent more time in the hospital than out during the past two years. And you think I have a problem? I've never missed a day of work or messed up a relationship. I've certainly never lost a fortune because I have yet to make mine. Look at these people. Just look at them. Some of them have red, blotchy faces. Some have the shakes. Their clothes look like last week's Goodwill special. I don't have anything in common with these folks. Maybe someday I'll be a psychologist for patients like them. Only they're the ones with the problem. Not me!" He turned to leave.

Mary had taken all she could of this impertinent young man. She couldn't keep quiet any longer.

"Oh, let's hear it from Mr. High and Mighty! I've had enough of your holier than thou routine. We aren't all the stereotypical lying in the gutter type of drunk. You seem to think the rest of us are charity cases who've reached the end of our ropes. And then you condescendingly imply that someday you may take pity on us. That you might deign to reach out a hand to help us provided we pay you to be our psychologist. You condescending son of a bitch. You've got drunk just like the rest of us. You've had problems because of it or you wouldn't be here. Am I right, Mr. Know It All?"

Brad liked Mary. She was usually quiet. She listened when anyone needed to talk to someone. He couldn't be rude and walk out on her. He walked back over to his chair and sat down.

"Mary, I may have spoken out of turn because I was mad at the counselor. I still think some of my problems are minuscule compared to some of the problems experienced by several in this room. I've never had DTs, never had a DUI, or a positive drug screen. I've never passed out in public. I don't drink alone. Therefore, I can't be an alcoholic. It's as simple as that."

The counselor broke in, "Just what have you had? What brought you into the hospital?"

"Well, my own two feet did, of course!"

Several of the group chuckled at Brad's comeback to the counselor's question. Others were still glaring at him like they'd enjoy tearing him up into little pieces. May he'd better try to level with them.

"Seriously, I had a bit of a personality clash with a professor of mine. Just because he'd seen me get drunk at several parties and because my grades were dropping, he took it upon himself to suggest I get treated for chemical dependence. He said if I didn't go into treatment he'd turn my case over to the dean. I can't afford for that to happen. You don't last long in graduate school with things like that on your record."

The group was listening but he still saw several blank stares in the room. They weren't following him.

"Don't you see? I had to come in here or kiss my education good-bye. So I agreed to spend a month in here during this first summer session. That still doesn't mean I'm an alcoholic!"

Sue, the nurse who co-led the group with the counselor, shifted in her chair so she could face Brad more directly before she addressed him.

"Brad, I think I remember you blood alcohol level being 0.25 when I admitted you. The legal level indicative of intoxication is 0.10 or higher.[1] People with levels of 0.10 have trouble walking, talking and perceiving.[2] I know you weren't talking coherently when I admitted you. And there's another thing. Your professor told me that the last time you got drunk at a party and you refused to let friends drive you home. He was worried about you, so he followed you home. He said the police stopped you. You couldn't stay in your lane. They let you off with a warning for DUI on condition that you allow him to drive you the rest of the way home. Then the next day you didn't remember any of the incident with the police the night before. We call that a blackout."

He usually could stomach Sue, but now he found himself wishing she'd not bothered coming to work today. Turning towards her said, "I should have known you'd listen to that old geezer. A blackout? That's ridiculous. All the guys I drink with have things they can't remember that happened when they were drinking. It's part of normal social drinking on our campus. You know,

---

[1] Hutchinson, S.A. Applying the Nursing Process for Clients With Psychoactive Substance Use Disorders. In Wilson, H. and Kneisl, C. (1988) Psychiatric Nursing, Third Edition, Menlo Park, CA: Addison-Wesley Publishing Company, pp. 348-395.

[2] Ray, O. (1983) Drugs, Society & Human Behavior, St. Louis: C.V. Mosby Company.

the ‘manly thing to do.’ I'll admit I've been drunk a few times, but that doesn't mean I'm an alcoholic."

Everyone in the group was looking at him like they all knew a secret he didn't. Slowly it dawned on him that they all thought he was exhibiting denial. He leaned back in his chair. He'd said more than enough. He was going to sit the rest of this session out.

* * * * *

Later that afternoon, Bill the evening charge nurse, made rounds. It was just after supper. Most of the patients were out in the dayroom talking and drinking coffee and getting ready to go out to a neighborhood AA meeting. As he passed Brad's room, he noticed that the lights weren't turned on in his room and he was sitting staring out the window. His shoulders were slumped. He looked depressed. Bill decided to go in and talk to him.

Speaking as he entered Brad's room after knocking, Bill said "Hi, Brad. I was walking by. I noticed you sitting here staring out your window. You look kind of down. What's going on?"

Brad sighed. He needed to talk to someone, but he didn't know where to start. "Oh, I don't know. It's just that I've spent the last several years focusing on learning how to help others. Now, here I am with a chance to help myself. I'm blowing it. I'm so angry I can't see straight. I need help, but it's like I can't get help unless I say the magic phrase, 'I'm an alcoholic'. I'm not willing to do that."

Bill walked across the room and switched on the bedside lamp before sitting down in the chair at the foot of Brad's bed. Once he was seated, he put both elbows on his knees and leaned forward towards Brad.

"Well, wanting help's a start. Maybe it's not important whether you label yourself an alcoholic. Maybe what's important is owning that you have a problem and being willing to do something about it. You know this is the first time I've heard you sound like you were even close to doing that."

Brad stopped staring out the window. He sat down on his bed and pulled his legs up and sat cross-legged in the middle of it. He looked Bill straight in the eye and began talking.

"There's that word 'problem' again. I get so defensive when I hear it. I'm supposed to help others that have problems. I'm not supposed to have them myself. I'm supposed to be strong and deal with things all by myself. I just don't know if I can keep going on like this. If I keep putting on this strong facade and focusing on solving other's problems instead of facing my own troubles, I probably won't be able to much longer. I just don't know where to go from here."

Bill smiled. "Well, let's start with something I know you're familiar with. Let's start with defense mechanisms. We both know they're unconscious and that they serve to decrease anxiety.[3] We're all human beings. Even if our job is helping others, it's only human nature to fall victim to denial and projection when it comes to looking at what we view as our own shortcomings. Having a drinking problem is not a personal failure. It's a symptom of disease. Alcoholism is a disease."

Brad grimaced. I" know. But it's one I don't have. I can't afford to have it. What kind of a psychologist would I be if I was an alcoholic."

Bill chuckled. "Probably a damned good one. There you go again. Classic denial. Excerpt I think its getting harder and harder for you to keep your denial in place."

Both men were quiet. A flock of birds descended on the lawn outside Brad's door. In the distance, he could hear the sound of a siren. Maybe Bill was right. He turned away from the window to look at Bill again.

Bill kept quiet. He didn't want to cut this period of silence short if Brad was filling it with some honest thinking. Even though he looked like he was trying to accept what he'd just said to him, he still looked like he needed to hear something else. Finally, Bill said. "Let's try another angle. What's the worst thing that could happen if you decided you were an alcoholic or that you had a drinking problem?"

Rolling his eyes and sighing, Brad answered. "That's too simplistic."

Bill continued. "Humor me. Let's go with this."

Brad glanced up at the ceiling. Then he looked back at Bill before saying, "OK. Uh, uh .... people would think I was a nothing but a no-good drunk. And I'd never get to drink again."

Bill smiled. They were on to something here. "And what would that do?"

After thinking a minute, Brad answered, "Well, I wouldn't have a social life. I couldn't dance .... not comfortably, anyway. I'd be uncomfortable in a lot of situations. I'd never enjoy getting loaded again, I'd ...."

---

[3] Hutchinson, S.A. Applying the Nursing Process for Clients With Psychoactive Substance Use Disorders. In Wilson, H. and Kneisl, C. (1988) Psychiatric Nursing, Third Edition, Menlo Park, CA: Addison-Wesley Publishing Company.

Bill interrupted. "You'd never have to wonder how you got home again. You'd never have a hangover again. You'd never have to face a cop asking you to walk a straight line again after he pulled you over. You'd never have an accident that hurt someone else or yourself, and on and on and on."

Sighing, Bill turned and looked out the window. Turning back, he began talking in a subdued tone.

"Maybe you're right. But I'm having a hard time relating to the folks in here. It's even harder at those smoky, crowded AA meetings. They're just a bunch of redneck old drunks. I find myself wanting to tell them to stop laughing at the chaos they've made out of their lives. I find myself wanting to tell them to 'get real' and to be serious."

Bill leaned further in towards Brad. "And?"

Brad continued, "Well, I spend half my time being angry as hell at them and the other half wanting to help them."

Bill nodded his head as if he was affirming what Brad was saying. Then, with a note of triumph in his voice, he said. "Ah, ha! The truth comes out. Listen to yourself. If you were your own patient, what would you say you were doing right now?"

Brad looked at Bill quizzically. Then he replied, "I don't understand what you mean."

Bill clarified, "What defense mechanism are you using right now?"

Brad's hands clenched. "Oh, you thing I'm projecting my problem with alcohol on to them?" That's too simplistic. Damn it! This isn't a case of simple projection."

Bill said. "OK. It's not simple projection. You're angry at what you see in them that reminds you of yourself. You're angry at them because they remind you of what can happen to you if you don't do something about your drinking. Seeing it all as their problem and wanting to help them instead of seeing your own problem and focusing on helping yourself is a form of projection. Your anger and your condescension both serve to keep it their problem instead of yours."

Brad glanced out the window again. Most of the birds had flown away. He hated to admit it, but it sounded like Bill had something here. Maybe he could use some humor to lighten things up. All of a sudden he felt real tense. He chuckled and said.

"Hey, Bill, wait a minute. Aren't you supposed to wait for me to have some insight instead of telling me your version of 'how it is' and what I'm feeling? Give me a break."

Bill sat up in the chair and stretched before answering. "There you go with the defense mechanisms again. Shall we try a mixture of denial and intellectualization this time? Perhaps a little minimizing with a dash of sarcasm and humor. We don't have that kind of time. Your life and your health are at stake here. Think about what I've said. As they say in the AA program, 'take what you like and leave the rest'. If you honestly don't think it applies to you, then ignore it."

Bill stood up and smiled as he laid what looked like a business card down on the table beside Brad's bed.

"I've got to go now. Remember that as long as you stay mired down in using defense mechanisms to keep from feeling your feelings and doing something about what's bothering you, the longer you'll be stuck knowing you're in pain but not knowing what to do about it."

After Bill left the room, Brad turned back to looking out the window. It was getting dark. He felt really down. What did Bill think I'd been sitting here doing besides thinking? He had some nerve, but he did leave me some things to think about.

He got up off the bed and walked over to close the blinds. The card Bill had left caught his eye and he reached for it instead. It was a wallet-sized folded yellow card. AA's twelve steps were printed on the front. Inside there was Hazelden's guide for a daily moral inventory. Then Bill glanced at the back side that Brad had left facing up. On it were the words, "God grant me the serenity to accept things I cannot change, courage to change things I can, and wisdom to know the difference."

He glanced out the window. There was a squirrel climbing a tree. Right now he wished he was that squirrel. Then things would be simpler. This was the pits being so fed up with the mess you'd made of your life that you want to change places with a squirrel. Glancing up he saw the first star of the evening begin to twinkle.

Before he caught himself, he launched a prayer of his own to whatever there was the kept the stars, the squirrels, and mankind itself going. He found himself sending out the thought: "Well, I reckon I could use all the things mentioned in that prayer. Right now I need some help focusing on 'change'. I've got a lot of changing to do, and I know I can't do it by myself. Please help me."

Then his mind was quiet. Several seconds passed before he was aware of staring at his reflection in the window. He was surprised to see a calm, relaxed person looking back at him. Maybe this is what the AA folks meant by the term "acceptance" they used over and over again. Maybe he was beginning to get close to that other word they used a lot, "serenity". He smiled at himself before he turned to walk out of his room. If he hurried, he could catch up with the others and make it to that AA meeting.

Chapter IV

I WANT IT NOW

Tracy pulled the unit door shut. She fought the wind to get it shut. The cold wind had been blowing at her heels ever since she left home to come into work. The cold and the dark were two things she didn't like about working nights. In nursing school they hadn't told her how hard it would be working nights once she was a nurse. There was a lot they hadn't warned her about. For instance, they had neglected to tell her that with your first job you'd have to make concessions. One of them was rotating shifts. Another was floating to different units. That meant she was working a lot of night shifts and on a lot of different units. It meant fighting the cold and the dark--- and a strong urge to go back to bed --- just to get to work every night.

She hung up her coat and put her things in her locker in the lounge. Before going to the conference room to hear report, she headed for the nurse's station. This was her first week on the chemical dependence unit, and she'd come in a little early so she'd have time to meet with the outgoing staff. She hated relating to a tape recorder. They didn't answer questions like live people did. So far she kept having lots of questions every time she sat through change of shift report.

She was aware of the hum of the overhead fluorescent lights as she entered the nurses' station. There was a bank of charts against one wall and cabinets across both sides and the back of the room. At the front of the room were desks and countertops surrounded by a window that looked out over what she'd learned everyone called the "day room". She turned away from the window and walked toward the table in the center of the work area where a LPN sat charting. The RN sat at one of the desks at the front window transcribing orders. They hadn't heard her come in, so she cleared her throat. They both looked up from their work to look questioningly at her.

She explained quickly, "Hi, I'm Tracy. The new graduate nurse assigned to work on this unit this week on the night shift. I came in a little early so I could talk to you about the patients."

The RN stared at her. Then she looked down her nose as she said. "Talk to us about patients? You'll hear it all on the taped report. We're busy right now, we have to get our charting done so we can get out of here on time. Since you're here, you can count with Nancy. That's Nancy, she's our LPN. She's in charge of giving all our medications on the evening shift. I'm Ms. Corrigan. I'm the evening charge nurse. I doubt if I get done here in time, but if I do, maybe then I can answer a couple of your questions."

Ms. Corrigan quickly turned back to her work after talking to Tracy.

Tracy felt dismissed. She sighed. Nobody had said this was going to be easy. Then she walked towards Nancy with her hand outstretched so they could shake hands. Nancy didn't reach for her hand. Instead, she looked her up and down before asking.

"Are you that new BSN graduate they hired to work relief around here? I'll warn you now, most BSN grads have a hard time of it here. We expect you to pull your own and not be continually asking questions. At least those ADN grads know what they're doing. Sit down. I'll be through with this in a minute. Then we can count meds."

Tracy sat. For the second time that night she felt dismissed. She realized that Nancy didn't even value her enough to expect her to answer her initial question. Things were going just great. She decided not to confront either Nancy or Ms. Corrigan with their rudeness. That would have created more problems that she'd have time to solve in the short week she was scheduled to work here. Besides she knew the only way to gain their respect was to show them she was a good nurse by letting them notice the kind of job she did.

Later both Ms. Corrigan and Nancy had gone home. Ms. James , the night charge nurse and Perry, the night LPN, had come in a few minutes late. They introduced themselves to her as the co-workers with whom she'd be working. Ms. James was reserved, but friendly, Perry was superficially friendly. Ms. James had assigned her medications for the night. She explained it was common practice to give any "relief" person this assignment if they weren't going to be assigned to the unit for more than a few days.

Perry seemed to resent having to interrupt his studying to make rounds every 30 minutes and checking on all the patients throughout the night, and Ms. James seemed comfortable relating to charts. She kept stuffing them with all the new forms the next day's shift would need to use for each patient, checking the transcription of orders for accuracy, catching any errors made during the day and evening, and talking to the occasional patient who got up for a smoke.

Tracy had to admit, the routine of stocking, giving and charting medications had been somewhat comforting. It relieved a lot of her anxiety about what to do if a chemical dependence patient got angry. She'd heard in report that some of them tended to be very hostile and demanding. There was one in particular, Mr. Jones. He was withdrawing from heroin, and although he'd been through the worst of it, he was still somatasizing --- complaining repeatedly of his multiple aches and pains and GI problems. The nurse who taped report also mentioned that he was very demanding. They'd let him take a long nap on the evening shift. She'd laughed on the taped report and joked that this was his new therapy .... that it was very 'nurse friendly' because it kept him out of their hair.

She was just ready to take a breather from checking all the medication orders against the kardex, when there was a loud knock at the medication window. She hurried to open it. A tall, thin man stood before her with his hands clenched in front of him. She started to say "Can I help you?"

When he interrupted her. "Where's my sleeper? I want it now. I can't sleep, and it's the only thing that'll help. The other nurse always gives it to me as soon as he's out of report. What's wrong with you? Why are you so slow?"

Tracy decided to respond tactfully. She smiled, "I'm sorry, I didn't catch your name, Mr. ...?"

The man answered. "Jones. It's Jones. Now gimme it."

Tracy spoke matter of factly, "Just a minute, Mr. Jones. I'll check and see what the doctor has ordered for you."

She turned away and walked back to the medication cabinet where she'd left the kardex. As she was checking the orders, she heard Mr. Jones loudly say. "Come on. What's your problem? All I need is my sleeper!!"

Tracy found that Mr. Jones' doctor had ordered chloral hydrate 500 mg. PO HS PRN sleep. As she turned back to Mr. Jones, she noticed that he was still dressed in his street clothes and that he was smoking a cigarette. She knew that nicotine from the cigarette would initially act as a stimulant[1] and make it even harder for him to go to sleep. She remembered her psychiatric clinical instructor talking to them about what to do when patients requested sleeping medication. She'd said to have the patients try to get to sleep on their own before giving them sleeping medication. She'd said that oftentimes they'd surprise themselves and go to sleep without having to be medicated. Consequently, they'd be less likely to become dependent on sleeping medications. All of these thoughts were going through her mind as she approached Mr. Jones.

---

[1] Ray, O. (1983) Drugs, Society & Human Behavior, St. Louis: C.V. Mosby Company.

"Mr. Jones, I understand your desire to go to sleep. However, it looks like you haven't tried yet to go to sleep. Why don't you put the cigarette out and go to bed? I'll make a deal with you. If you lie there for thirty minutes without going to sleep, come back and I'll give you the PRN sleeping medication your doctor ordered."

She mentally held her breath as she delivered this speech to Mr. Jones. She found herself wanting to back away from him. The expression on his face was one of incredulity.

His expression quickly turned hostile. He pounded his fist down on the medication window ledge. "Are you deaf and dumb, bitch? How many times have I said 'gimme it now'? Read my lips, GIVE ME MY SLEEPER NOW!"

Mr. Jones' tone of voice rose with every word. He was practically yelling at her. Ms. James came hurrying over. She took one look at the situation and said, "What's going on here? You two are making enough noise to wake the whole place!"

Before Tracy could answer, Mr. Jones exclaimed, "I don't know where you got this new nurse, but I always get my sleeper first thing. It's already almost midnight and she hasn't given me my pill. Now she says I have to try to sleep without it first before she gives it to me. If you don't make her hand it over, I'm reporting you both to the head nurse tomorrow. If I have to, I'll go all the way to the top. I'm sure someone in administration would like to hear how you're violating my patients' rights!"

Ms. James turned to Tracy. "He's right, dear. He always gets his sleeper at the beginning of our shift. There's an order to cover it."

Tracy took a deep breath. Her first night on the unit and she'd hit head-on with a manipulative patient who had already successfully set up her charge nurse to take sides with him against her. Her instructor had called that sort of manipulative behavior "splitting staff against staff". She'd said the way to handle it was to set firm limits and for staff to enforce them consistently. She'd also said it was important for staff to support each other so a manipulative patient couldn't manipulate the situation to meet his or her needs by capitalizing on the conflict he'd generated between the staff members. What should she do? She couldn't lecture her charge nurse.... especially not in front of a patient.

She looked towards Ms. James hopefully. "Could you and I talk privately, Ms. James?"

Ms. James rolled her eyes and sighed. "I'm really busy, this patient needs his medication, and you want to talk. OK, but make it snappy."

They walked out of the office and across the hall to a conference room. Ms. James stood facing Tracy with her hands on her hips. She looked upset, and as Tracy closed the door so the patient couldn't overhear their conversation she realized her mouth had gone dry from her anxiety. She swallowed a couple of times before saying.

"Ms. James, I heard in report that Mr. Jones is manipulative. I was taught that the best way to handle a manipulative patient is to set firm limits. They also taught me that you should never give a sleeper to someone who hasn't yet tried to sleep. They said if you did, you'd be helping them become dependent on sleeping medication. This is especially true for a recovering addict. That's why I asked Mr. Jones to try to sleep before I gave him his sleeper."

With every word, Tracy's voice got softer, and she spoke more slowly. This was because she was looking at the frown on Ms. James' face get deeper with her every word. By the time Tracy finished her explanation, Ms. James' frown had become a full blown scowl.

I can't believe you're telling me how to take care of a drug addict...you're still wet behind the ears, and I've been doing this for years. I don't know where you got your training, and frankly, I don't care. If you'd been in this business as long as I have, you'd know what works and what doesn't. I don't need no high falutin' new grad coming in here and telling me how to run my shift. Now, before I write you up for insubordination, I want you to go out there and give Mr. Jones his medication. Do I make myself clear?"

Tracy gave up any hope of reasoning with Ms. James over Mr. Jones' sleeper. She had to work with the woman, and it wasn't worth jeopardizing her job to make any more of an issue of it at this point.

After giving Mr. Jones his sleeper, Tracy somehow managed to make it through the rest of the night. She and Ms. James were careful not to talk to each other any more than they had to for the rest of the shift. Tracy stayed busy so she'd keep her mind off the earlier incident and confrontation with Ms. James.

* * * * *

However, as she was driving home from work, she kept focusing on the dilemma of Mr. Jones and his automatic PRN sleeping medication. She'd tried the direct approach and that hadn't worked. She'd like to be able to just forget it, but she couldn't. That wouldn't help Mr. Jones...or any of the other chemically dependent patients who repeatedly manipulated the staff into giving them sleeping medication whether they needed it or not. Tracy was glad she had a couple of days off. She had an idea that she'd need the time to think this one through.

When Tracy returned to the chemical dependency unit after her days off, she found herself working the day shift. Ms. Prinz, the unit manager, always seemed busy. At times Tracy thought she should talk to her about the incident. Then every time she'd walk toward Ms. Prinz' door, she'd think of several reasons why she shouldn't. Finally, on her third approach, Ms. Prinz looked up from her paper work.

She asked, "Yes, may I help you?"

Noting Tracy's reluctance, she added, "You're my new relief nurse aren't you? We haven't got a chance to visit together yet. Why don't you come on in and tell me how your orientation to this new unit has been going."

Tracy smiled as she walked into the office and sat down. Maybe this was going to be easier than she'd thought.

"Well, for the most part, OK. There's one problem I've encountered, and the direct approach to solving it didn't work. Now I don't know what else to try."

Ms. Prinz took a sip of her coffee and looked thoughtfully at Tracy before she said, "Why don't you tell me about the problem. Maybe we can try to work out the solution together."

Tracy found herself telling Ms. Prinz everything that had happened the night she and Ms. James had the disagreement about Mr. Jones' sleeping medication. She was unable to tell Ms. Prinz' reaction to what she was saying because there was no emotion registered on her face. When she finished, Ms. Prinz sighed and poured herself another cup of coffee.

"Tracy, what they taught you in school was right. You've got to learn to work with people so they don't feel like they have to be defensive. Ms. James is a good nurse. Most of the time she's one of the best nurses I have to work constructively with manipulative patients. However, since she transferred to nights, she refuses to treat demands for medication as manipulation. I've talked to her about it. She thinks that refusing such demands and dealing openly with them as manipulative behavior would result in creating loud and hostile situations when the staff isn't there to handle them. Besides, she thinks its more important not to disturb the sleep of the other patients who are sleeping. In a way, she's right. If you'd continued to deny Mr. Jones' demands, he might have become louder and even violent."

Tracy looked thoughtful before replying. "Ms. Pinz, I kind of see that. However, I'd like you to focus more on what you said about me learning to work with people. What did you mean?"

Ms. Pinz paused. Then she answered.

"Let's start with this. It's important to treat someone who has worked longer than you have with a certain level of respect. Life's lessons may have taught them things that your classes and books didn't cover. You can learn from other people's wisdom. Even if they're wrong, if you come across like you know it all because you're fresh out of school --- whether or not you mean to --- they'll usually get defensive. Perhaps, if you'd been less direct and asked her to consider Mr. Jones' behavior as manipulation and to please share any suggestions for handling it appropriately, she might have reacted differently. Approaching her like that would have acknowledged her seniority and her experience. Chances are she would have found herself working with you instead of against you."

Tracy got up to leave Ms. Pinz' office. She looked thoughtful.

"I think I'm beginning to see what you mean. I'd like to talk to her tomorrow morning before our shift starts. Maybe I can get her to help me. I'm sure she has some good ideas."

Ms. Pinz smiled at her and replied, "I think that would be a good idea."

* * * * *

The next morning Tracy approached Ms. James and said, "I'm sorry we started our relationship the way we did. Do you have a few minutes to talk to me about what happened?"

To her surprise, Ms. James readily accepted her invitation. When they'd found a private place to sit down, Ms. James started their conversation by saying, "I was kind of hard on you the other night."

Tracy found herself interrupting her, "I know, but in a way I think I had it coming. I must have sounded like I didn't think you knew anything. I'm sorry. I know you've had lots of experience, and I didn't mean to step on your toes. I didn't even give you a chance to tell me why you thought it was better to give in to Mr. Jones' demands."

Ms. James grinned. "That one's easy, child. We don't have a lot of staff on at nights, so if he had got violent ... and he has several times ... we might have had trouble controlling him. Then, too, if he'd got any louder, he would have been waking the other patients up. Sometimes you have to weigh the therapeutic benefit for most of the patients against the benefit for one patient."

Practically thinking out loud, Tracy commented. "I still don't know what to do about Mr. Jones' demanding, manipulative behavior. We might be enabling cross addiction to sleeping medications. How could we work together to solve this problem without risking a situation that would wake the other patients or set up Mr. Jones for a violent outburst?"

Looking thoughtful, Ms. Jones replied, "Well, let me think on that one. It would need to be a way that didn't make him feel singled out or picked on. And if we could use peer pressure to our advantage, it would help. Of course, if we do something using peer pressure, it would need to be on another shift when the patients are awake."

While Ms. Jones continued to look thoughtful, Tracy thought over what she'd just said. She realized it made a lot of sense.

The she noticed a look of triumph unfold across Ms. James' face as she exclaimed. "I've got it! I'll stay over for community meeting this morning so they know you and I have a united front on this thing. Then we'll talk about manipulation being a symptom of the disease of chemical dependence. We'll point out that it's in their best interest to begin looking at their own manipulative behavior and to work on changing it. Then we will talk about how non-manipulative behavior is actually more effective, and we could give them lots of examples. When they start to realize that manipulation doesn't work as well for them as they thought, we'll start talking about how they can help each other with this problem. Then, we can talk about examples of manipulation on the unit and how they can address it as a group. One of the examples we'll talk about is demanding sleeping medication when you haven't honestly tried to sleep. Then we'll tell them that from now on no sleeping medication will be given to anyone that hasn't tried to sleep. We'll do some patient teaching about the dangers of cross addiction. We'll ask them to help us to enforce the "try to sleep first policy." We'll ask them to help us to use community meetings to confront any member of the community that ignores this policy and becomes loud and demanding after people have gone to bed."

Ms. James added, "You'll find that as a group they're very good at using peer pressure to protect the good of the group. If wanting to keep things quiet for everyone after they've gone to bed isn't enough of an incentive for them to use peer pressure in this situation, then we'll add to the incentive. We'll tell them there will be no television viewing allowed during free time until everyone complies with this rule. That should do it."

Tracy's mouth hung open. Then she closed it and said, "Isn't that a little extreme? Does that violate patients' rights?"

Ms. James laughed. "Oh, no. Television is not a human right. It's an earned privilege. As such, it is often very effective in shaping behavior. I should have thought of this approach before. I just didn't think beyond my shift, and this is the first time anyone has offered to work with me on this problem. Thanks."

* * * * *

Two weeks later, Tracy again found herself working with Ms. James on the night shift. She was assigned medications again. No one asked for a sleeping medication except one person. Ironically, it was Mr. Jones. This time he had his pajamas on, and he'd spent the past half hour trying to sleep, but he hadn't been able to fall asleep. This time he politely asked for the medication, swallowed it, said thank you, and returned to bed.

Tracy charted the medication and looked up to see Ms. James smiling at her as she said, "Well, Tracy, thanks to you and me getting our heads together, it looks like no one's demanding to be given sleeping medications before they've tried to sleep on their own anymore. Everyone but Mr. Jones complied with the new unit rule after our community meeting. It only took one free time without television before Ms. Jones' peers convinced him to comply. What's more, Mr. Jones seems to be really working on changing some of his other manipulative behaviors. Our plan really worked. And now, all we have to do is review the policy in community meeting whenever we get a new group of folks. You did good, kid!"

Chapter V

SHE SHOULD KNOW BETTER

It was just a little after 7:00 AM. Morning report had just started. It was Monday, so there was a lot being said about how different patients had done while being out on therapeutic leave over the weekend. Suddenly, my ears perked up. Margie, a female alcoholic patient had met up with Paul, a married male alcoholic patient, over the weekend while they were both out of the hospital on therapeutic leave. They'd made quite a weekend out of it. Not only did they use together, they'd slept together.

" Oh no," I thought, "and she'd been doing so well."

The charge nurse pressed the stop button on the tape recorder.

"Can you believe that?" she said. "He was on his way to making it this time. He was working hard on making a go of his marriage and his sobriety. And this tramp had to come along and spoil it for him. His poor wife."

Mary, a co-worker, spoke up saying, "Their cheating on his wife was one thing, but they also both relapsed. I thought they were both going to make it this time. You kind of expect that from a guy, but she should know better."

I was stunned. I thought Mary was an objective, caring professional. How could she expect women to be immune to relapse while expecting men to be prone to it?

I decided to keep my thoughts to myself. I left report to make rounds. Heaven knows we have a busy day ahead of us. I didn't need to waste time getting into a difference of opinion with my co-workers. I stopped by Margie's room last so we could talk a few minutes before I had to attend staffing.

Margie was looking out her window. Her bedroom light was off. It was hard to see in the shadows, but her face appeared drawn, and it was obvious she hadn't bothered to dress yet. She looked so dejected. I knocked on her door before entering; she didn't even turn to see who it was as she tonelessly said, "Come in."

I entered her room. "Margie, it's me, Cassie. I just heard in report about your weekend. I'd like to hear your version of what happened before I go into staffing."

I pulled up a chair next to her bed, and leaned towards her as I spoke.

Margie sighed, "I'd rather not talk about it. What's done is done. I blew it. I never meant to drink again, and what happens? First chance I get, I drink. What's worse, I ended up waking up in a motel with Paul. Cassie, I don't even remember going to the motel. What's wrong? Am I going crazy?"

"Margie, you're not going crazy. What you're describing sounds like a blackout. A blackout is a common symptom of your disease. When someone like you drinks, they sometimes appear to function normally when they're drinking, but they forget big chunks of what they did during that time.[1] It doesn't mean you black out. It just means you are unable to remember a chunk of time or what you did during that time. So its no wonder you don't remember how you ended up in that motel."

Margie still looked upset and dejected. "Is that supposed to make me feel better? I feel like a fool. Like I'm wasting my time even kidding myself I'll ever sober up. Even when I think I'm going to make it, I still manage to throw caution to the wind and end up drinking again. Why did I do it Cassie?"

I maintained eye contact as I replied, "Margie, you have a disease. Knowing why is not as important as figuring out what you are going to do about it. Yes, you had a relapse. You drank. You were out of control. You did some things you can't remember and that you wish you hadn't done. The important thing is you came back to the hospital. That means you are back on the road to recovery. Remember that the program teaches you to take one step at a time....one day at a time. Today you are in the hospital and sober. What's passed is passed. Learn what you can from the mistakes and then let go of it. Recovery means focusing on the solution, not on the problem. If you truly accept that you are powerless over alcohol, then you can accept what happened as further proof that you are powerless. Once you've done that, you should be able to taker AA's other 11 steps to recovery."[2]

Margie sounded angry as she lashed out. "You sound like a damn commercial for AA. You sound like Mona, my sponsor. AA is all I ever hear from her."

---

[1] Burkhalter,k P.K. (1975) Nursing Care of the Alcoholic and Drug Addict. New York: McGraw-Hill.

[2] Alcoholics Anonymous (1976) Alcoholics Anonymous: The Story of How Many Thousands of Men and Women Have Recovered from Alcoholism. Third Edition. New York: Alcoholics Anonymous World Services, Inc.

Then she was quiet. Her shoulders sagged. She took a deep breath. Quietly she continued, "You're probably both right. Maybe I should give her a call after breakfast."

As I stood up to leave, I said, "Good idea. You need to focus on your recovery, not your relapse. I bet Mona will help you do that. I've got to go to staffing now. I'll check back with you later."

Margie followed me to her doorway and flipped on her light switch. As I started down the hall, I noticed she was looking through her closet for something to wear. Good, that meant she was ready to face the day.

I hurried into staffing. Dr. Blount was already there as was the social worker, nurse manager and the unit's two alcoholism counselors.

"Good, Cassie. Glad to see you could finally make it. Would you close the door? We've been waiting on you."

That was my greeting from Dr. Blount. I closed the door and sat down at the conference table across from Ms. Thornton, my nurse manager. We exchanged glances. I could tell she was about as pleased with Dr. Blount's attitude as I was.

Dr. Blount started the meeting by saying, "I think we need to review Margie's case first. Evidently, she had quite a fling this weekend with Paul. I'll be meeting with Paul and his wife this afternoon to try to undo the damage Margie created when she seduced Paul into playing around and relapsing. Lets hear what everyone has to say about her case. We need to consider discharging her. She's a detriment to the other patients who are here and are serious about their recovery."

Susan, the social worker was the first to respond. "Dr. Blount," she said, "Margie has no where to go. She has no job, and no way to provide for her two children if we let her go now. Her mother as agreed to keep the children, but only if Margie remains in treatment and later goes to a halfway house. It'll open up in about two weeks. It would probably be best for Margie if we used those two weeks to help her work through this relapse."

Dr. Blount looked both doubtful and thoughtful. Ms. Thornton cleared her throat, and began talking, "It sounds to me, doctor, like you want to punish Margie by discharging her from treatment before she's ready. Would you kick a diabetic out of the hospital just because he ate a candy bar?"

Dr. Blount frowned and replied, "Don't be ridiculous, Ms. Thornton. This is an entirely different matter. I've been working very closely with Paul for several weeks now. He's just reconciled with his wife. He's hooked up with an AA sponsor, and he's really got a chance to make it this time. What you don't realize is that this patient poses a real threat to Paul's sobriety and his marriage. If she stays here, it'll be much harder for him to make it."

It was now or never. I had to speak up. I cleared my throat. Everyone looked my way. "Dr. Blount, it sounds to me like you think Paul is as addicted to females as he is to alcohol. Maybe he does have a problem with sexual acting out, but that's his problem, not Margie's. Both patients are responsible for their own behavior and relapses. Paul's recovery and marriage don't depend on whether Margie continues to be a patient. Paul's recovery depends on his willingness to work on his own issues. It's not fair to view Margie as a seductive impediment to Paul's progress. Both patients relapsed , both have problems. Hopefully, both will have an equal chance at recovery. If you discharge Margie before she's ready, then that won't be true. She'll be a victim of yet another sexist bias."

The room was hushed. Dr. Blount's face was red as he replied, "Well, we've heard from the feminist section. Thank you, Cassie. We'll hold the applause. Now, if you don't mind, please refrain from interrupting again with such nonsense."

Jim, one of the counselors, came to my defense. "Cassie has a point. Let's not make a gender issue out of this. Both patients have relapsed, both deserve a chance at recovery, and both deserve to remain in treatment. I've been working with both of them in counseling sessions. I'm convinced that Margie is motivated to stay sober. This was a temporary setback. Paul seems somewhat less motivated, but it wouldn't be in his best interest to discharge him at this point, either."

I was grateful Jim had spoken on Margie's behalf. If I'd said anything else, Dr. Blount might have just dismissed it as more feminist rhetoric. I reminded my self that I needed to tone down my input in the future. Obviously, my not doing so had just put Dr. Blount on the offensive.

After staffing, I walked into the dayroom and found Margie hanging up the phone. She was smiling.

"That was my sponsor. She told me about the time she relapsed. She's had a few blackouts too. She's been sober 20 years. I'm beginning to believe I can follow in her footsteps. Thanks for helping me decide to call her."

Margie's smile was contagious. She was back on track. She was once again pursuing her recovery one step at a time.

Chapter VI

HOME AWAY FROM HOME

Molly sighed as she hung her jacket up in the closet. She wondered what Peg and Chuck were doing right at this moment. Peg had probably got home off the school bus about 4:00 PM, and Chuck had probably got in from work around 6:00 PM. Mavis probably went home after putting dinner on the table for them. She could just see the two of them sitting there eating, trying to be cheerful and pretending that everything was normal. Only it wasn't. They were there, and she was stuck 200 miles away in this treatment program. Chuck and her mother-in-law had convinced her she had a drinking problem and that she needed to do something about it.

She'd agreed for Peg's sake. Every child deserved a sober mother. Molly had to admit she'd not been sober very often in the two months before she came into the treatment center. Chuck hadn't directly threatened her with divorce if she didn't seek treatment, but she knew the threat would become real if she pushed him any further with her drinking. She loved Chuck, and she adored Peg. She couldn't let this disease force their family apart. She sighed again as she realized once more that she needed to be in treatment. She really didn't have a choice. She just wished she wasn't so far away from home.

She suddenly looked at her watch. If she didn't hurry, she'd be late for the "Lights out, Sleep Tight" group meeting. She rushed out of her room, turning out the light as she went. Her roommate, Mary Beth, had already left for the meeting. In the hallway she ran into Sally who was rushing to the same meeting. They smiled at each other.

Sally said, "Can you believe how they've got us trained to go to meeting after meeting all day long? Our days are one solid string of meetings. Sometimes I think if I hear the Serenity Prayer one more time I'll throw up. Then, there are other times that hearing it feels like a hug from some cosmic Teddy Bear. What do you think?"

Walking into the meeting room, Molly answered, "I know what you mean. I spend half my time resenting all this structure and half of it being grateful for it. I think I'd go crazy without it. I know I'd probably get too anxious worrying about everything and start drinking again."

Pete, the evening counselor, smiled at them as they took their seats. Inez, the nurse who co-led the group was busy talking to Charles, a patient who had just entered treatment that morning.

Pete greeted them with, "Glad you could make it ladies. Let's get started. Molly, you've been here almost two weeks now. Why don't you explain to Charles what this meeting's all about?"

Molly responded, "Great, that's what I get for being the last one in the door! Seriously though, I don't mind. This meeting is our wrap-up meeting for the past 24 hours. That means we all talk about how our day went and whether we met our goals for the day. This daily review helps us live one day at a time. It forces us to take a 'daily inventory' of all that we've done and felt. Pete says this helps us learn to practice AA's 10th step that advises us to take a personal inventory on a regular basis and to acknowledge when we've made mistakes.[1] Once we've all shared our daily inventory we all participate in a group relaxation exercise. It's easy to get to sleep when we leave the group and return to our rooms and our beds. Actually, some of us to sleep and snore away during the relaxation exercise."

The group laughed at her remark about snoring. Molly found herself responding positively once again to the group's easy-going camaraderie. She belonged here. These people knew her and accepted her as one of them. They were really tough on each other at times, but that toughness was motivated by genuine concern and understanding.

* * * * *

Early next morning over breakfast Molly found herself sitting at the table with Mary Beth and Charles. Charles looked like he was feeling pretty edgy because he was going through withdrawal. He was quiet, and he answered Mary Beth's questions with the fewest words possible. Molly couldn't help remembering how uncomfortable she'd been when she stopped drinking. It had been difficult to talk to others when she'd felt that badly. If the others had left her alone to stew in her misery though, she'd probably have checked out against medical advice and run scurrying home to Peg and

---

[1] Alcoholics Anonymous (1976) Alcoholics Anonymous: The Story of How Many Thousands of Men and Women Have Recovered from Alcoholism. Third Edition. New York: Alcoholics Anonymous World Services, Inc.

Chuck. The others had kept talking to her. Finally they'd broken through her misery and got her attention. Gradually she'd come to trust them. Now she knew that they were the reason for her staying here and for her staying sober. Hopefully they'd be a big part of the reason for her keeping things that way.

She found herself saying to Charles what had been said to her. "I know things are tough right now for you. Hang in there. It does get better. You're going to find yourself caught up in a whirlwind of structured activities. Of course, all this group pressure occurs when the last thing on your mind is talking to a group of strangers. I sat where you are sitting a couple of weeks ago. Half the time I wanted to die because I felt so bad. Mostly I just wanted to leave and go home and pretend none of this had ever happened. People kept talking to me anyway. The only way I could get them to go away was to talk back to them. They wouldn't let me get away with just talking about the weather. They wanted me to talk about what was going on in my head and how I felt. I finally realized that what I first thought was badgering was really their way of showing me they cared and of helping me. They wanted me to get better right along with them. That's what I want for you Charles. I want you to get sober and clean right along with the rest of us."

Molly couldn't believe she'd made such a long speech. If nothing else, she'd just convinced herself to keep talking to her peers.

Charles didn't even look up during Molly's sale's pitch for peer interaction. He just wanted to crawl in a hole and die. Who was this broad trying to snow him with this Polly Anna bullshit? Maybe if he didn't answer her she'd just go away. Couldn't she see he was miserable? Who asked her to interfere anyway? He put his napkin down on the table and started to scoot his chair away from the table. If he left, this broad would have to leave him alone. Before he made it up out of the chair there was a new intrusion into his 'personal space'.

"Mr. Samuels, sit back down a minute. I'm Ms. Parsons, the nurse assigned to you today. I need to talk to you a minute. I wanted to go over today's schedule with you before you left breakfast so things wouldn't be quite so confusing. Keeping up with all these meetings can be overwhelming at first. Can I sit down and go over this with you now?"

So much for skipping out. Charles knew he had to make a favorable impression on the staff if he was ever going to get out of here so he forced himself to smile. "Sure."

Ms. Parsons sat down and handed him a copy of the schedule. She pointed to the first item on the schedule and said. "This is our first meeting of the day. We call it our focus meeting. Someone reads from a meditation book, and everyone takes turns responding to the meditation. They also share their goals for the day. The next meeting is what we call our 'gender group.' Men go to a men's group, and women go to a women's group. In these groups people share problems they're having getting sober that are affected by their sex. For instance, women have more problems related to arranging childcare while they are in treatment than men generally do. Men often have more trouble getting in touch with and expressing their feelings because our society has taught them it's not the 'manly' thing to do."

Ms Parsons finally paused to take a breath, and as she did, she noted Mr. Samuels' facial expression. He looked uncomfortable. Suddenly, she realized that in her hurry to explain things to him before the first meeting started, she'd gone way too fast. She was crowding him. She'd better put the patient's need before her own here and slow things down a bit. She took time to take a sip of her coffee before smiling and slowly asking.

"Do you have any questions about these first two meetings?"

Charles thought for a couple of seconds. He finally decided to try the honest approach.

"No, but they seem kind of silly to me. I came in here to stop drinking ---- not to learn how to be an emotional blubbering fool whose every action is driven by a list of goals."

He grimaced as he pronounced the word, "goals". It was obviously not one of his favorite concepts.

Ms. Parsons never missed a beat. "I know it all seems strange and silly in the beginning. Bear with us Mr. Samuels. We know that these approaches work. These activities are the things that help people learn how to stay sober and clean. Let's go on to the third meeting, the one that's before lunch. This is an educational group. In it we focus on teaching you about your disease and how to recover from it. We cover all sorts of topics from how to change habits and ways of thinking to ways you can adapt your diet to support your sobriety"

Charles glared at Ms. Parsons. She wasn't getting the message that he just wanted to be left alone. To hell with making a good impression. Sometimes a man had to do what he had to do.

"Are you telling me I have to spend three solid hours in this stupid activity shit before I get a chance to be alone and eat lunch?"

"In a way, I am. Isolation --- separating yourself from others --- is a common component of alcoholism. Hiding ourselves and our drinking from our friends soon causes us to stop relating to other people altogether. Pretty soon we don't know how to relate to other people unless we're drinking with them. It' s important for us to help our patients learn to relate to others because they've often forgotten how. So, yes, we do everything we can to keep our patients involved in group activities. Besides, keeping busy keeps them from being alone and focusing on how bad they feel."

Charles smiled. He had her now. "I heard you slip a couple of times and say 'ourselves' and 'our'. Are you trying to tell me that you're an alcoholic?"

He felt so confident this last question would throw her that he backed his chair out from the table and started to stand up.

Ms. Parsons smiled. "Yes, I suppose I am. That's besides the point. What's at issue here is you and your recovery ---- not me and mine. Now, let's get back to going over this schedule."

That gave him food for thought. She was an alcoholic. Maybe she did know what she was talking about. Maybe she'd been through this. He sat back down in his chair and scooted it back up to the table. Maybe he should listen to her. He leaned towards Ms. Parsons with renewed interest. He noticed the hint of an acknowledgment of his acquiescence cross her face as she continued her explanation of the day's schedule.

"After lunch we have a two hour block of recreational activities planned. The first hour is for creative expressions. It focuses on some form of creative group effort to make something. Sometimes we get involved in music therapy instead. In music therapy we use music to help get in touch with and express feelings we're having. The second hour is for some type of physical exercise: aerobics, walking, tennis, swimming, etc."

Charles rolled his eyes, cleared his throat, and interrupted. "There you go with that feeling thing again. I just want to stop drinking. I'm not into this 'feely-touchy' California shit. I'd rather just get down to basics so I can get this over and get the hell out of Dodge."

There, that ought to take care of her and her attitude.

Wrong again. Ms. Parson's tone got even more assertive as she continued. "These are the basics. This is how you get the hell out of Dodge. You are here by choice. If you can't tolerate the program and can't commit to full participation in it, then you need to think about leaving so we can devote our time to someone who is serious about wanting to get and stay sober."

The room got quiet. He'd done it now. He’d finally got her dander up. He knew if he blew this treatment gig, he'd be out of a job. He'd better play the game and go along with this "know-it-all" nurse.

"OK, OK. I get the picture. What's next on your precious schedule?"

"From 3-5 PM people either meditate and do the step work assignments their counselor has given them or they meet with their counselor. Usually your counselor will have an intensive 1:1 counseling session with you every other day. On the other days he or she will just be checking with you briefly on how things are going with you. On those days a nurse will spend the remainder of the two hour period with you. The nurse will supervise your step work assignments and answer any questions you might have about the 12 step program, recovery or your disease in general. Do you have any questions?"

Charles sighed. They had everything worked out. He'd never get alone time away from these people. "No, I don't suppose it'd do me any good if I did. I can tell that I can't talk you out of this blessed schedule so hurry up and finish explaining it. I don't have all day. "

Molly found herself chuckling again. She'd been just as resistive, and she couldn't help but enjoy this display.

Ms. Parsons smiled. "That's just the point. You do have all day. It's filled with precious time. We're going to help you learn to use that time to your advantage. Back to the schedule. Molly seems to be finding this all quite amusing, so I'm going to ask her to explain the rest of it."

Molly almost choked on her coffee. She'd done it to herself again. Oh well, here goes. "OK, after the work sessions, we have an hour off for dinner just like we did for lunch. You'll be delighted to find that we always eat our meals together as a group. Look around you. You'll notice that people from our unit are in groups together around these 3-4 tables. After dinner we return to the unit and have a community meeting. In that meeting we focus on dealing with issues related to being a patient on our unit. We talk about things like keeping the unit clean, following the rules, who's bothering whom with what, etc. Then we go off-grounds to a community AA or NA meeting as a group. Sometimes the AA or NA meetings come to us "

Charles' interest perked up. "You mean we get out of this joint and actually go somewhere?"

"Sure, almost every night. One or two nights a week people from the community come here for a meeting. On the others we go out to meetings. If you're thinking of sneaking a drink, an AA meeting is one of the hardest places imaginable to get away with it. Besides, we're closely supervised. After the AA or NA meeting we return to the hospital and have our "Lights Out, Sleep Tight" meeting. I won't explain that one because you sat in on it last night. What did you think of it?"

Charles answered. "It was different. I missed the last half of it because I slept through most of it. You guys had to wake me up to get me to go to bed."

Mary Beth had an impish grin on her face. She chimed in with, "Charles, I think you just solved your problem. There's at least eight hours out of every 24 that you can be alone, and that's when you're sleeping!" She and Molly both chuckled.

Charles glared at both of them. "Thanks a lot. What do you two broads know about anything anyway? I'm glad you find all of this so damn amusing!"

Molly quickly got serious. "I apologize for laughing. Once you've been here awhile, you'll see that we all laugh a lot. It helps us deal with the pain of our past and to push us along from day to day. You'll learn to welcome it. We're rather like a family here. We tease each other, we laugh, we cry. We serve as a kind of sounding board for each other as we try out new ways of thinking and acting. In a way this has become our 'home away from home.' I hope that you'll come to see it that way too, because then it gets easier to be here. Sobriety seems more real when you've got that kind of group support behind you."

Later when the lights were out and Molly was drifting off to sleep, she chuckled to herself. She just realized she'd been feeling sorry for herself and had let herself get homesick, and today she'd begun to accept being here. Trying to convince Charles that he needed to become involved in the treatment program made her see how much this place and these people had come to mean to her. It was just like her to come in through the back door. In trying to convince someone else, she convinced herself. She didn't have to be homesick anymore.

Chapter VII

PROMISES KEPT and RECEIVED

Gerri knew this was the only chemical dependence treatment center in town that her insurance covered. She knew that she was only here because she'd agreed to come so her case wouldn't be reported to the Board of Nurse Examiners for disciplinary action. She didn't want her diversion of narcotics at Broadway General Hospital where she'd worked as a nurse reported to the Board. That was until they asked her to take this prolonged "vacation". She'd agreed to participate in the state's peer assistance program for nurses and to seek treatment because it seemed the lesser of two evils. Now she wasn't so sure. She remembered having been here as a student nurse as part of her psychiatric rotation just a little less than a year ago. That meant if there were still students here from her alma mater, they'd probably recognize her. That was all she needed on top of everything else. That would mean that in spite of all her efforts, everyone would know what had happened to her. She'd be ruined in this town.

Chilling thought. With an effort she turned her attention back to the nurse who was admitting her. It was such a shock being on the patient side of this procedure. She was having trouble concentrating and answering the nurse's questions. She'd actually missed the nurse's last question. She leaned forward towards the nurse and forced herself to say, "I'm sorry, what was that?"

The nurse repeated. "What and how much were you using before you came to the hospital?"

Well, that was direct enough. It would be easy to lie. God knows she'd been lying to herself and her roommate about her addiction. Lying probably wouldn't work this time since she'd given them a chain-of-custody urine specimen for a drug screen as soon as she'd walked in the door. She might as well be honest because the lab results would give her away anyway.

"I was shooting up several times a day with 300 mg. of Demerol. When I got up in the morning, half-way through my evening shift, and when I got home. I even had a seizure a couple of times. Thank God, I was always home when that happened. Good thing my roommate was a nurse too so she knew what to do."

The nurse was busy writing down her answers on the admission form. This seemed to be old hat for her, but it wasn't easy for Gerri to be this honest. After all, since she was a nurse too, she knew she was supposed to role model a healthy life style. She was supposed to take care of the sick. It went against everything she'd ever learned about her profession to put herself in a position to be taken care of herself.

Now here she was having to make these embarrassing admissions that were going into her permanent medical record. She felt like she was throwing her life away, and the nurse who kept asking these probing questions and writing down her life's secrets looked cold, distant and bored. Gerri realized she was going to learn a lot from being a patient that she could use to improve her own practice of nursing. That is if she ever got to go back to work.

* * * * *

Later that evening she stood in line for her bedtime medications along with the other patients. She started worrying again about students showing up from the school from which she'd graduated. Maybe her fears were groundless. Maybe those students didn't come here for clinical experience any more. After she'd swallowed her pills, she asked the RN who was giving medications, "Uh, I was wondering, do students from St. Patrick's still come here for their Psychiatric rotation?"

The RN paused before answering, "That used to be your school, didn't it? I can understand why that would concern you. If you'll wait until I finish here, I'd like to take a few minutes to sit down and talk to you about that."

Gerri agreed. As she turned away she couldn't help resenting the fact that she really did have to worry about them recognizing her. The nurse wouldn't have answered her the way she did if that wasn't the case. Gerri had just sat down with a cup of coffee when the medication nurse approached her and introduced herself as Celia. She went on to say, "I've got a little time now. Why don't we find an empty office so we can sit down and talk about this."

Gerri followed her into an empty office and sat down before she glanced across the desk towards Celia. As she pulled her cigarettes out of her pocket, she asked, "Mind if I smoke?"

The nurse was quick to answer. "Actually, I do. We're basically a non-smoking building. That's a JCAHO requirement now, and we have to comply with it if we want to keep our accreditation. Smoking is allowed outside on the grounds, but it's not allowed anywhere within the walls of the hospital."

Even though this wasn't the answer she wanted to hear, Celia's matter-of-fact tone and caring manner kept her from getting angry over the refusal. No small feat. If anyone had told her she'd calmly accept being told she couldn't smoke, she would have laughed in his or her face. Amazing what taking on patient status did to a person.

She had to admit she was beginning to accept being a patient to a certain extent. She still knew how to be assertive and take initiative though. They'd wasted enough of her time without giving her a straight answer about the St. Patrick's students. She looked directly at Celia before saying in her most professional manner, "You didn't answer me earlier when I asked about the student nurses coming here from St. Pats. Now I'd like a straight answer if you don't mind."

Celia was quick to respond, "Like I said earlier, I appreciate your concern. I realize you were a student there and that you're worried someone from there will recognize you. The answer to your question is yes. Students from St. Pat's are here every Monday and Wednesday. That means they'll be here tomorrow morning."

Gerri let out a big sigh and rolled her eyes. "Great, just great. What do I do now?" Gerri nervously tapped her fingers on the desk. She really needed that cigarette now. In answer to her question, Celia reached into a desk drawer, pulled out a form and handed it to Gerri. Just what she needed at a time like this, Gerri thought. Another frigging form to complete. Trying to get a straight answer from these people was like pulling teeth.

Celia noticed Gerri's resentment so she quickly explained, "This is a confidentiality statement that visitors, students, and all employees must sign before they can work with patients. It's a legal agreement to maintain confidentiality about anything related to the identity of patients they encounter in our hospital. Once they sign this, they're legally bound not to discuss your identity or case outside of the hospital or with anyone not directly involved in your treatment experience."

Gerri had heard all of this before. She remembered signing one of these forms when she was a student here. She leaned towards Celia and said. "I'm familiar with the form. I signed one when I was a student here. It's easy to sign. It's much harder to rely on a mere piece of paper to protect your career and your reputation. This is a real risk for me."

Celia replied. "Let me ask you something. When you were here as a student, did you see anyone that you knew?"

Gerri thought that one through. Then she answered. "Well, yes. There was Mr. Gillis, my old high school math teacher. "

Celia continued her soft questioning. "And did you find yourself tempted to tell anyone about Mr. Gillis?"

Gerri thought a minute and replied. "Uh, yeah. My parents. He's still their neighbor. I thought they should know that they'd been trusting an alcoholic who lived next door to them as an upright, upstanding citizen all these years. What a joke."

Celia quickly cut in. "Gerri, can you hear yourself? Can you detect your attitudes about alcoholism coming through here? You sound like you think substance abuse is a moral problem that someone chooses as some sort of indecent self-indulgence. That's got to make it hard for you to accept yourself in your present circumstances. Please realize that addiction is a disease. It's not a question of moral choice, right or wrong, good or evil. Anyway, let's get back to your reaction to seeing Mr. Gillis here when you were a student. You mentioned you were tempted to talk to your parents about him. Did you?"

Gerri felt her eyes tearing. Celia had really hit the nail on the head. She was having trouble accepting herself as a drug addict. Her attitudes about poor old Mr. Gillis were perfect examples of how she felt about herself when she was honest about it. Enough. She needed to answer Celia's question.

"No. I never did. I thought about it a long time. I realized that ethically I couldn't say anything. At least, not if I wanted to live with myself in good conscience."

Celia nodded. "I think we're getting somewhere. Its important to realize that you respected Mr. Gillis' confidentiality even though you were tempted to tell your parents. Gerri, in all honesty, I can't promise you that all the students that show up here tomorrow will be as ethical and professional as you are. My guess is that they probably will be. Think about it. If you'd like, I can talk to Dr. May. I could get an order to make sure you're not assigned to any student nurses and that none of them be allowed to read your medical record. That will protect your confidentiality somewhat even though they'll still be in a position to recognize you."

Gerri liked that idea. "That sounds like a great idea. I hadn't even thought about them reading my chart. I couldn't handle that. I couldn't get into one of them working with me either."

Celia leaned forward towards Gerri. "Wait a minute. Consider the alternative. If you allowed a student to work with you that student could learn some valuable lessons about the reality of addiction as nurses experience it. They'd be exposed to the fact that we aren't immune to this disease just because we're nurses. Who knows, you might even have a chance to plant a seed in that student's heart and mind that could help them keep from developing their own addiction some day."

Gerri returned to her room and spent a night tossing and turning. She felt like she hadn't got any real sleep all night. This was a hard decision to make. On one hand, it sure seemed less risky to have a doctor put a "no-student access" order on her case and medical record. On the other hand, she'd made a real mess of her life and her profession. If she could help keep just one student nurse from doing what she'd done, it might help her start regaining her self-respect. She had to have a smoke, so she slipped out on the grounds for a quick smoke. The sun was just coming up, and the air felt cool and refreshing on her face.

* * * * *

After her smoke, she went back in to get her roommate. They walked to breakfast with the other patients. She passed a group of student nurses on the way. She couldn't tell for sure, but it looked like one almost did a double take when they passed on the sidewalk. Maybe she'd already been recognized. Over breakfast, Mike, an "old-timer" who had less than a week remaining before he was discharged confronted her.

"OK, Gerri. Truth time. You seemed happy enough when we started over here. Halfway here you clamed up. Come to think of it, you got quiet right after we passed those students. What gives?"

Mike was a perceptive old cuss. She appreciated his concern. She smiled.

"Not much. It's just that I went to the same nursing school they do. It's been less than a year since I graduated. I think they're going to recognize me. I think one already did. If they talk about me being here when they get back to the school, the fact that I'm in here as a drug addict will be all over this town in no time at all."

Mike started to answer when Phil leaned over and patted Gerri on the shoulder. He signaled to Mike to let him talk for a second. Phil had been in for about two weeks, and he'd talked about this time "taking" since this was his third try at treatment. Gerri glanced up at him when she felt his hand on her shoulder.

"Gee, kid. I know just how you feel. The first time I was in here we had some Girl Scout troop wander through the unit singing Christmas carols and handing our candy and oranges to all us 'poor old drunks'. One of the mothers with the group worked in my office. You could just see the light bulbs go off in her head. When I finally got out of here that time and back to work, you could hear a pin drop when I walked into that office. People were afraid to talk to me. It was like I had the plague or something. At least that's what it felt like. I found out later that they had all wondered what had happened to me until that mother came back with 'the scoop'. Initially they were horrified. How could their boss be such a lush? Then their dismay slowly turned into concern. They worried about my drinking ruining the business. None of them felt like they had any real job security anymore. They were afraid to do anything that might cause me to start drinking again."

Phil paused to take a few bites of his breakfast before continuing. "It took me several weeks to get them to stop 'treading on eggshells' around me and treat me like a regular person. I'm not sure they ever really trusted me again. That's why I ended up back in here these last couple of times. I just couldn't handle the stress at work. This time I've sold the business because I have to find something that works for me. I need a job where people accept me for who and what I am rather than treating me like I could fall apart and turn into some sort of monster at a moments notice. So, even though my case may be different from yours, I still think you need to be careful."

Gerri nodded her head and swallowed. "Great, just great. That's just what I needed to hear. I wondered what could really happen if people talked. Now I know."

Gerri sighed and took another sip of coffee. Then she turned towards Mike who was still looking at her with a concerned look plastered all over his face. He started talking to her again.

"So, that's what's got you worried. You're afraid these student nurses will go back to school and talk about seeing you here. You think once they do the whole nursing community will be gossiping about you being a drug addict. What makes you think you're that important to them? Let me tell you a little story about the last time I was in here."

Here goes, thought Gerri. Mike's really getting on my case.

Mike continued. "I had gone to great lengths to keep my alcoholism hidden from the folks at the office where I'd worked. When I was in treatment, I just knew they were going to find out somehow. I knew that was going to be the end of me. Then at one of the community AA meetings they took us to, it happened. The man sitting three chairs down from me was my immediate supervisor. I was devastated. What if he recognized me? Sure enough, after the meeting, he wandered over to talk to me. He was friendly and supportive. It wasn't until the next day that I figured out that I'd seen him there too. He was an alcoholic like me. The next time I went to that meeting, he led the meeting. To my amazement, when he told his story, I found myself identifying with him. Here was someone who'd been through what I had, who'd been where I'd been, and experienced some of the exact same problems. And he'd kept sober for several years. I figured out that he could understand what I was going through and that he could help me get sober like he had. I ended up asking him to be my sponsor. When I relapsed this last time, he was able to spot it quickly. Naturally, being my sponsor helped. Being my supervisor helped too. He noticed the difference in my job performance right away. He knew he had to get me back into treatment quickly before things got worse and I lost my job."

Gerri was confused. Finally, she said, "That's a nice story. What's the point? Are you suggesting one of these student nurses will end up being my sponsor?"

Mike laughed. "Hell, no. I'm suggesting that our Higher Power doesn't give us anything we can't handle. In fact, He gives us exactly what we need to help us recover. Let me quote from my Big Book[1] here, from pages 83-84. People in the program call these the promises. They are contingent upon our working real hard at complying with AA's 12 steps of spiritual living. It says: 'We are going to know a new freedom and a new happiness. We will not regret the past nor wish to shut the door on it. We will comprehend the word serenity and we will know peace. No matter how far down the scale we have gone, we will see how our experience can benefit others. That feeling of uselessness and self-pity will disappear. We will lose interest in selfish things and gain interest in our fellows. Self-seeking will slip away. Our whole attitude and outlook upon life will change. Fear of people and of economic insecurity will leave us. We will intuitively know how to

---

[1] Alcoholics Anonymous (1976) Alcoholics Anonymous: The Story of How Many Thousands of Men and Women Have Recovered from Alcoholism. Third Edition New York: Alcoholics Anonymous World Services, Inc.

handle situations which used to baffle us. We will suddenly realize that God is doing for us what we could not do for ourselves'."

Mike had read these profound words slowly and reverently in a deep, resounding voice. The whole table had stopped eating and listened to every word. There was a respectful silence when he'd finished. Gerri liked the sound of what he'd read. What's more she liked the way she felt after hearing them. Surprisingly, she realized she was comfortable with the fact that she'd inadvertently decided to let a student work with her by not giving the nurse a directive to get the doctor's "no-student access" order when she got up this morning. She leaned towards Mike and asked. "Mike, let me see that a minute."

He handed his Big Book to her. She took a minute to read them over and think about what they said. Then she asked Mike. "Does this mean that when I'm worried about someone blowing my confidentiality I'm being self-seeking and that I'm feeling sorry for myself? Does it mean that when I stop being selfish, I'll start using what I've gone through to help others? Does it mean that this thing you call a "Higher Power" will guide my every action and give me what I need to cope with anything that comes my way?"

Mike was chuckling. "Whoa girl. Slow down. Basically, that is what it means. Stop worrying and feeling sorry for yourself. Start focusing on using what you've learned to help others. When you do, you'll experience peace and serenity because you'll be allowing your Higher Power to guide all that you do. You'll feel free, and you'll be happy."

Gerri frowned. "This all sounds too good to be true, if you ask me. If these promises really happen, how come people relapse? What happened to you? Surely your relapse was a violation of these so called 'promises'."

Mike answered her slowly. "My Higher Power, whom I choose to call God, didn't let me down. He didn't take away the promises. I quit earning them. I quit working the steps. I stopped pursuing a spiritual pathway to daily living. I pushed all of that away. I couldn't handle the success or the progress I was making. I couldn't handle the positive feelings. I got into being selfish again. And all of the sudden being spiritual and serene seemed like silly, boring outcomes to pursue, I started feeling sorry for myself again and wanting to drink. I started worrying about my problems instead of focusing on solutions or on what I had to be grateful for. I stopped focusing on helping others. My own self-pity and worry were what let up to my relapse. I was the one that let myself down."

Gerri thought about what Mike had just said. "I think I'm beginning to understand what you're trying to tell me. At least I hope so. Before I came to breakfast, I conveniently 'forgot' to have the nurse get the doctor to put a student-ban order on my chart. Then when one of them seemed to recognize me this morning, I started regretting my oversight. I think you're right. I'm calmer when I focus on helping someone else that when I focus on my own selfish interpretation of my problems and get all tied up in worry and anxiety. I think that "Higher Power" of yours had you read those promises to me for a reason. They're helping me handle this situation, and it's definitely a situation I couldn't handle by myself. Thanks for sharing them with me."

Mike replied, "I really had no choice. I had to use my experience to help you. That's the only way I can stay open to receive the promises of AA's program."

* * * * *

Later that day, Gerri found herself waving good-bye to Jill, the student nurse who'd been assigned to work with her. It had been Jill who'd recognized her on her way to breakfast that morning. Things had been slightly awkward initially. By the time Jill was ready to leave, they'd both got over the initial awkwardness. Jill obviously admired Gerri's openness and honesty in discussing her addiction and her first hesitant steps towards recovery. Jill had promised Gerri that she'd jealously guard her identity and maintain her confidentiality. She'd promised to only use initials when referring to her patient in post conference and in written assignments. In fact, she'd even asked Gerri's permission to discuss details of her case in post conference. She'd explained she thought all her classmates could benefit and learn from Gerri's experiences. Surprisingly, Gerri found herself open up even more after she'd agreed for Jill to share the details of her experience in post conference. She realized what she'd gone through had the potential to help more people that way. She was amazed that just last night she'd been afraid of being recognized and now she wanted all of the students to hear her story. What a turn around. What's more, she was beginning to feel a sense of accomplishment and pride as she walked away from having waved good-bye to Jill.

Chapter VIII

NOT IN MY GROUP YOU DON'T

Ellen sat smiling as she pulled into the hospital parking lot. She'd been working as a pool nurse here one or two weekends every month on the chemical dependence unit to augment her low teacher's salary. Now that the university was on Christmas vacation she was finally going to get to work on a weekday. She was finally going to meet the treatment team she'd known only on paper these past few months.

She felt comfortable and at home sitting in report. Somehow taking change of shift report always made her feel more like a nurse than lecturing to students did. There was a charge nurse and a head nurse sitting in on report with her as well as a LPN and a psychiatric tech assigned to work on the unit today. She was usually worked weekends with only herself and a LPN on duty most of the time. What a difference being here on a weekday made!

The charge nurse assigned her to care for five of the 16 patients. Except the one who was being discharged later today, all of them were in Phase ll of the program. That meant they'd survived detox and their heads had cleared enough to allow them to start working on the psychiatric components of their recovery. They'd be participating in a lot of group work during the day. Ellen was looking forward to being in the groups with them as a co-leader. She'd learned how to do both individual therapy and group therapy in graduate school when she'd got her Masters in Psychiatric/Mental Health Nursing. Now she was going to get to put that education to use in a group setting once again.

She decided she'd better say something to the charge nurse because it didn't look like she was assigning her to co-lead any groups. "Excuse me, Ms. Downs. I was wondering if I could attend some of my patients' groups."

A fleeting look of surprise crossed Ms. Downs' face in response to Ellen's request. Ms. Downs quickly regained her composure and answered, "Why of course, dear. It's just that we ... uh ... we never have any of our nurses involved in the groups. The groups are all done by our drug and alcoholism counselors. I suppose you could attend. Of course, you'll have to ask the counselor that leads the group before each group starts. Why don't you start with just one group today. See how that goes. After all, if any admissions come in, you'll need to admit them, and I want you to be available to do that. It wouldn't do to have you tied up in groups all the time."

Ellen began her shift by taking vital signs and helping round up patients for AM medications. She also introduced herself to her patients. She'd got so busy helping take off orders, attending a staffing and answering the phone that it was 10:00 AM before she had time to think about attending a group. She checked the schedule and found there was a Human Sexuality Group scheduled for 10:30 AM in Conference Room B. The group was to be led by a Ron Peters, a Licensed Chemical Dependency Counselor. She approached Mary, the LPN assigned to medications, and asked her to point out Mr. Peters.

Mary put down the water pitcher she was holding and pointed towards a young man who was making his way down the hall. He had a Big Book in one hand and a cup of coffee in the other.

Ellen yelled, "Thanks, Mary!" over her shoulder as she hurried off to introduce herself to Mr. Peters. She caught up with him in the dayroom.

"Hi, Mr. Peters. I'm Ms. Sisney, and I've been assigned to work with several of the patients who'll be attending your Human Sexuality Group. I was wondering if I might attend also?"

Mr. Peters looked thoughtful. He'd never had this happen before. "Well, I guess you could. I'd prefer that you actively participate though if you attend. I've found that having an outsider just sit and observe often puts a damper on the group process. Of course, you'll also need to ask the group's permission once the meeting gets started."

Ellen smiled. "Thanks. I'd like to participate. Let me finish charting these vital signs and I'll be there."

* * * * *

Ellen had just walked into the conference room when Mr. Peters got up and shut the door. When he sat back down, everyone suddenly got quiet. Mr. Peters told the group that Ellen had asked to sit in on the group. He told them he'd told her she could as long as she participated and the group gave their permission. All eyes turned towards Ellen. She took a deep breath before saying.

"Hi, I'm Ellen Sisney. Some of you know me as the nurse that works on weekends sometimes. This week I get to work with you during the week.

Since I'm assigned to several of you, I asked if I could sit in on this group. I need to have your permission though before I do that. I know it's hard to talk about sexual issues sometimes. It gets even harder to do when there's someone around that you don't know."

To her relief, Ellen saw heads nodding. Perry, a male patient, who was community president spoke up.

"Thanks Ms. Sisney for asking. I'd like to ask the group for a show of hands so we can vote on whether or not we want to let an outsider into our group. OK, guys. Raise your hands if you're comfortable with Ellen joining our group today."

Glancing around the room, Ellen saw everyone raising their hands. She'd made the first hurdle.

During the first half of the group the group process was fairly superficial. Mr. Peters tried to get the group to talk about sexual issues they were having in their relationships with their significant others, but no one was willing to disclose anything that personal. Consequently, there was a prolonged period of silence that was finally broken by Mario whose wife had threatened to leave him if he didn't get help for his drinking. Mario had been discussing, with his therapist, a sexual problem he'd been having with his wife before he came into the hospital. He'd never discussed it with anyone else. However, maybe this was a safe place to talk about his problem.

Mario cleared his throat before he broke the group's silence. Everyone looked at him expectantly. He swallowed, and his voice wavered slightly as he said, "Well, I guess I can talk about this here. It's hard to talk about, you know. It's really been bothering me. I don't know what to do about it."

Ellen had spent some time with Mario earlier. They'd already formed a rapport together. He'd already begun to trust her and to disclose some of his feelings and concerns to her. Therefore, she felt confident in responding to him now. She leaned toward his and softly asked, "What's been bothering you Mario?"

She noticed his hand clench and unclench before he spoke. "I think the medical term for it is im ... imp ... impotence."

There, he'd finally said it. He looked down at the floor. A couple of the men in the group laughed nervously. They quit abruptly though when they saw that Mario couldn't even look at the group, he was so embarrassed.

Slowly Ellen continued. "Mario, impotence is a common problem that happens to most men at one time or another. Why don't you tell us about your problem with it. Maybe someone here can share how they coped with a similar experience after you tell us about yours."

Mario looked around and saw that no one was laughing. Almost everyone was looking at him with concerned expressions on their faces. Slowly, Mario opened up and began to talk to the group about his problem with impotence. Two other men in the group responded by telling him how they had coped with their impotence. One of the women talked about how she and her husband had worked through a brief period of impotency her husband experienced. The group got so absorbed in helping Mario that they were surprised when Mr. Peters reminded them it was time for the group to end. He also thanked everyone for participating in the group. Ellen spoke up and summarized the group's process for the session.

In closing, she asked. "Do you realize even though sex is a difficult topic to discuss several of you risked talking about your personal experiences with impotence and how you overcame them? Your willingness to take that risk helped Mario know that his problem is not unique. You let him know about several things he and his wife can do to help work through this problem. You are to be commended for caring enough to risk such personal disclosure. Thank you."

As they left the group, Mr. Peters asked Ellen to meet him in his office for a "debriefing session." His surprise seemed genuine as he exclaimed, “You were really good in there, Ellen. It was more than you just being comfortable with the topic. You were confident about what you were doing; it showed. You did a great job."

Although Ellen appreciated Mr. Peters' candor, she felt like he was being somewhat condescending. Therefore, she responded in a like manner. "I've taught Human Sexuality. When I got my Master's degree in nursing, I spent lots of time learning to be a group therapist. I am confident about what I did in the group. I'd be worried if I wasn't. By the way, you were surprisingly good yourself."

Later, Ellen met with Ms. Downs to analyze the post-group exchange she'd had with Mr. Peters. She told her, "He was genuinely surprised that a nurse wanted to sit in on the group. He seemed amazed that I could function therapeutically during the group. I don't think he was intentionally trying to antagonize me."

Ms. Downs smiled apologetically. "Our nurses haven't had the education you have. The only groups they go to are patient education groups. You're what I call the 'new breed' of nurse. When you really get down to it, you've probably got more education and experience with group process than most counselors do. I bet you did give him a run for his money. The counselors here act like all nurses can do is hand out medications, chart, and answer their questions about how to document things properly. It'll be interesting to see what happens during the rest of this week now that they've encountered a different sort of nurse."

* * * * *

When Ellen came into work the next morning, she found a notice on the bulletin board signed by the unit's program director. It announced that nurses could no longer participate in group sessions. It also said that all patients were to be referred to their counselors to discuss their psychiatric concerns. The notice explained that the counselors found it disruptive to the group's progress to have nurses attend groups. It advised nurses to stay within the boundaries of their job descriptions and to attend to nursing duties rather than interfering with issues of therapy.

Ellen sat down. She hadn't expected to start a "turf war" with the counselors. She didn't see herself as posing a threat to what they considered their job. She thought they'd overreacted. They had essentially gone over the nurse manager's head to the Program Director and declared war by having it mandated that nurses couldn't do what Ellen had been educated to do. Ellen knew that getting patients to disclose and process their feelings and concerns was essentially a nursing function. In fact, Ellen considered it the main focus of psychiatric nursing. She doubted that most drug and alcoholism counselors had the psychiatric background that she did. She knew they hadn't had the physiological background. It would be impossible for them to approach patients holistically because they lacked the basic physiological knowledge necessary to do so. If nurses couldn't work as full partners with the rest of the multidisciplinary team, a valuable component of the care afforded patients by the team would be missing. Something had to be done. The question was, what?

* * * * *

Ellen sat back in her chair and peered out the window. She was sitting in the conference room with the head nurse, the program director and a counselor. They were waiting for Mr. Peters to arrive. Ellen had talked Ms. Franklin, the unit's nurse manager, into calling this meeting so they could openly communicate about the territorial issues that had surfaced when she participated in the Human Sexuality Group. Ms. Franklin was receptive to the suggestion because she was angry over the posted memo. She didn't like it when people didn't go through channels and went over her head to the Program Director. She thought the Program Director had over stepped the boundaries of his job description. She didn't think he had any business dictating what nurses could and could not do. She had wanted to confront the counselors and the Program Director with the inappropriateness of their behavior. Ellen had finally convinced her that escalating the turf battle wouldn't be in the patients' best interest. They had to work together as a team if they wanted to meet patient needs effectively. Taking an angry, hostile, defensive stance wouldn't promote the kind of team work they needed to have on this unit. Finally, Ms. Franklin had agreed to set up a meeting where all parties could negotiate a solution to their problem.

Mr. Peters walked in ten minutes late. The first words out of his mouth were. "So, we meet again Ms. Sisney. Here to shake things up a mite again are we?"

Ellen could see that she needed to diffuse the situation. She said. "It was never my intent to 'shake things up'. Nor was it my intent to take over your group. If that is how I came across, I apologize."

Ms. Peters was obviously surprised that Ellen had apologized so quickly. He rapidly shifted gears and responded, "Apology accepted. I realize you didn't intentionally try to stir up problems for us. However, you came on like gangbusters in that group. Then you had the audacity to inform me that you were an expert on both human sexuality and group process. You insinuated that I knew very little about either. I realize you have extensive education and experience. You need to realize that some counselors have equivalent education and experience. It's also important for you to know there are no masters' prepared nurses on our full time staff. If we allow you to set a precedent, then we'll have nurses running groups who have no understanding of what they're trying to do. The result could be disastrous for patients."

Before Ellen could reply, Mr. Brasewell, the Program Director spoke up. "Mr. Peters is right. That's essentially why I posted the memo about nurses not getting involved in groups and leaving therapeutic issues up to the counselors."

Ms. Franklin didn't let Mr. Brasewell continue. She interrupted saying. "Ellen has told me that she was actually impressed with what she observed in the group. She wasn't critical of Mr. Peter's leadership. She felt like his compliment to her after the group was condescending, and she responded by becoming defensive and condescending in turn. I can understand Mr. Peters being upset about this, but he should have come to me with his concerns rather than going to you. I don't like being left out of our chain of command. I strongly feel that decisions like the ones you posted that directly effect the nurses that work on this unit should be made by nurses. At least we should be invited to have input into making them."

Ms. Franklin suddenly stopped. She was remembering that she'd agreed to try to diffuse the situation and to promote team work. After a moment, she continued. "Can't you see that what initially happened here was a momentary personality clash? There's no need to let this little spat divide us into warring camps. We can talk about communication issues and administrative channels of authority later. What we need to do now is to focus on how we can resolve our differences and work together as a team."

She paused before continuing. "Everyone, including our patients, will be losers if we continue to invest our time in trying to win this "I'm a better therapist than you are" game. We need to work together, and we need to view our patients holistically. Nurses' have a medical background that prepares them to do just that. Because of their medical background and knowledge they can spot and handle a lot of important things. Like when someone is starting to go into DTs or has had a stroke. Granted, counselors have more experience counseling patients than nurses do. However, I'm convinced after talking to Ms. Farwell that we need each other. We need each other's background and knowledge to compliment the expertise that each discipline lacks. We have to work together and share our knowledge and expertise if we want to give our patients the care they deserve."

The room was suddenly quiet. Mr. Brasewell had never heard Ms. Franklin say so much at one time with so much conviction. Mr. Brasewell and Mr. Peters exchanged looks. Then they simultaneously glanced at Ms. Sisney and Ms. Franklin.

Mr. Brasewell was the first to speak. "You're probably right about that Ms. Franklin. Our disciplines and our patients do need all of us working together as a team."

Mr. Peters leaned towards Ellen and said, "I'm sorry if I sounded patronizing after that group. I didn't realize then that your background had prepared you to conduct groups and one-to-one therapy sessions with patients. I still think it would be a mistake to let other nurses without a similar background start participating in our groups. Besides, you'll be going back to your teaching job in another week or so."

Ellen noted that Mr. Brasewell was nodding affirmatively in response to Mr. Peters' comments. Then she said. "Mr. Peters, I've thought about that. I think it would be ideal if the nurses and counselors on this unit started working together a bit more than they now do. If a nurse and a counselor worked together in a group, then that nurse could learn about how to handle a group from the counselor and from the experience of being in the group. That would eventually mean less work for the counselors. It would also mean having a co-therapist in every group. Having a co-therapist enhances the quality of the groups."

Ellen paused before continuing. "More importantly, it would also open up a professional relationship between the two disciplines. That would mean sharing the benefit of our mutual and separate areas of expertise. I know you'd like to know if one of your patients vital signs were escalating and indicating he or she was starting to go into withdrawal. Sure you could eventually see the shakes. Knowing about the vital signs would let you know much sooner. You'd be able to get the patient medicated in time to prevent the occurrence of DTs. Similarly, nurses would like to know when a patient has had a fight with their spouse and is at greater risk for suicide than he or she has been because of it. Counselors find things like that out in the counseling sessions they do and in the groups. Opening up the groups to both disciplines and opening up our communication of what both disciplines knows couldn't help but enhance patient care on all sides. The patients will gain by our cooperation. And, if we continue to further oppose each other, the patients will lose."

Everyone in the room was nodding their heads in agreement. Ellen began to relax. Maybe there would be a chance for this unit to develop some real team work after all. She smiled and stood up as she said, "Well, I have to leave to go get my medications passed. I want you to realize I know that I'll be back in the proverbial 'ivory tower' before long, but I'm looking forward to working with you as part of this team until that time. I appreciate you allowing me to do so."

When she had left the room, Mr. Brasewell said, "Well, maybe we needed a little prodding to begin to do some things a bit differently around here. She has a point. We can learn from each other's knowledge and experience. We can probably work better together than we could separately."

Ms. Franklin quietly spoke up. "Thank you for coming this morning, gentlemen. Perhaps it took this experience to help us realize that Ellen is right. It's our patients who stand to lose if we can't work together. Now, let's get out there and get back to work. By the way, I've decided to sit in on this morning's group so I can begin to learn how to work with you in that arena also. When my charge nurse runs this afternoon's medication teaching group, I'd appreciate it if one of you would attend. That way you can begin to learn about the side effects of the medications our patients are on. Then you'll know when you need to tell us if you notice anything that indicates a patient may be having a medication related problem."

Mr. Peters and Mr. Brasewell stood up. Mr. Peters politely opened the door for Ms. Franklin. The three were smiling as they left the conference room. The last thing Mr. Peters said to Ms. Franklin as he got on the elevator was. "Ms. Franklin, you have a deal."

Chapter IX

A MODERN DAY FAIRY TALE

A heavy November wind blew across her face as she struggled with the door. Mindy finally got it pulled closed. On her way to work she'd caught the weather. Snow was predicted, and she certainly wasn't looking forward to its arrival. She pulled her scarf off as she walked down the hall to the women's locker room. It was still dark outside. She hated coming to work when it was still dark.

Wanda was already in the locker room. Seeing Mindy, she called out. "Hey, Mindy, did you hear what happened? The hospital may be in a lot of trouble now. They refused treatment to a lady a couple of nights ago because she didn't have any insurance. She ended up dying in jail. She had to detox there since they don't do detox at the State Hospital anymore. The State Investigative Committee released a press statement that they'll be investigating the incident. What do you think?"

Mindy sighed before answering. "That's awful. I felt badly yesterday when they told me they'd had to turn her away in the middle of the night because she didn't have any funds. I know they gave her a thorough physical evaluation before they turned her away and that she hadn't started withdrawing at that time. I wonder if she'd still be alive if they'd been able to admit her?"

Wanda said. "I know. This is all so unfair. Everybody's bummed out about it."

Putting her things away in her locker, Mindy remembered talking to Bryan about the case yesterday evening over supper. He worked in marketing at the hospital, so it hadn't been like she was breaking a confidence. Bryan tried to get her to look at the hospital's viewpoint.

"Mindy, you've got to remember it's a corporate hospital. It's not a non-profit organization. Even if it was, it couldn't afford to give away charity beds. Psychiatric hospitals are in economic crisis right now. Two of them have already closed down. The competition is just too fierce. All of the negative media coverage has compounded the problem. How many medical hospitals do you know of would admit people who walked in off the street requesting medical care if they weren't in medical crisis and had no insurance?"

She hadn't any answers for him. They talked about health care systems a lot because Bryan had gone back to school to major in health care administration and Mindy had been a psychiatric nurse for over two decades. Bryon had already convinced her that the day of free medical care had passed, the United States health care system was in dire economic straits. With more and more people unable to afford insurance, it was inevitable that more and more people would be doing without health care unless something was done to fix the health care system.

When she'd gone through nursing school, she'd been taught every human being had the right to access health care regardless of his or her economic situation. She remembered the halls of the Catholic hospital where she'd got her training being crowded with over-flowing beds that the crowded wards couldn't absorb.

A strong undercurrent of humanitarian philosophy had flavored most of what the nuns had taught them about nursing. What had happened to that value system where need took priority over ability to pay for medical care?

Wanda opened the lounge's door and said, "Hurry up, sleepy head. They'll start report without you if you don't get the lead out."

Mindy just shook her head and headed for report. Later, after report, she sat in on staffing. A good part of the meeting focused on Ms. Towers, an alcoholic who'd been in treatment for about a week. She'd finished detoxing and was getting involved in other aspects of the treatment program now that she was neurologically capable of concentrating for short periods. The team was deciding how to discharge her and still meet her healthcare needs. They didn't want to deplete the woman's insurance benefits completely with this single hospital stay. They knew now that her head had cleared, she could start benefiting from group sessions. She'd need to internalize their content so she could face living in the community without relapsing.

Mindy asked Dr. Basinger, Ms. Towers doctor. "Did the managed care representative say anything about Ms. Towers' outpatient benefits? If she could get plugged into our aftercare program, she could still get what she needed from group sessions."

Dr. Basinger responded. "Well, that's a good idea. Only thing is she's already used up her quota of outpatient chemical dependency treatment benefits the last time she was here. She did OK for a while, but when her husband died she relapsed."

Ms. Moran, the head nurse, spoke up. "You know," she said, "all of this insurance mess is because the insurance companies refuse to accept chemical dependence as an illness. You don't see them refusing treatment to a diabetic who goes into insulin shock because that diabetic already used up their 'treatment quota'."

Dr. Basinger nodded affirmatively before saying. "You're right. But their side of it is that the chemical dependence treatment sector took advantage of liberal reimbursement policies for years. Consequently they've had to rigorously re-structure their policies to prevent further unnecessary losses. Who knows where chemical dependence treatment will eventually end up."

Mindy responded, "Most, if not all of it, is already being done in outpatient settings on both coasts. Inpatient chemical dependence treatment as we know it will be a thing of the past.

* * * * *

Later that afternoon, Mindy approached Doctor Basinger in his office. "Dr. Basinger, I heard something at a workshop last week that gave me an idea. There's this treatment center in northwest Arkansas for women who are chemically dependent that offers a quality 30 day program for only $500.00. Why can't we get Ms. Towers transferred to that treatment center?"

Dr. Basinger looked surprised. "You've got to be kidding. That's half of the cost of one day at most places. Where'd you say that place was?"

After making several phone calls, Dr. Basinger was able to contact the rural treatment center. They had an opening at the beginning of next week. Dr. Basinger asked them to hold the bed for Ms. Towers. Now all they needed to do was help Ms. Towers come up with the $500.00 and a way to get to the treatment center.

Mindy was caught in traffic driving home. Suddenly the idea hit her. What if the hospital held an impromptu fund raiser. She bet the local radio and TV stations would be glad to give them free air time to announce the affair. It was ironic, but now that someone had died in jail after being turned away from a hospital, they were "hot news". It was certainly worth a try.

The next day Mindy talked to the treatment team about her idea. They decided to hold a community dance in the gymnasium on the upcoming Saturday night. One of the interns was a member of a band that played nightclub gigs on weekends. He volunteered his band to donate their time.

Mindy and the other nurses went all over the hospital and all over several other hospitals putting up posters announcing the benefit dance. They also left posters and "collection jars" at strategic cash registers all over town. They made sure everything they posted identified the purpose of the fund-raiser without disclosing the patient's identity. The marketing team went all out too. They appeared on every community affairs talk show offered in the greater metro area during the remainder of the week. The weather even cooperated: the predicted snow never came.

Mindy and the other nurses personally attended change of shift report on all the hospital's units. They collected over $100.00 from the nurses. The interns brought in another $100.00 from the medical school. They got almost $200.00 from the collection jars they'd distributed. It only cost $100.00 to decorate the gymnasium for the dance. One of the local restaurants volunteered to cater the affair.

* * * * *

Mindy and her friends came in early Saturday afternoon to decorate the gymnasium. While they decorated, it began snowing. Several inches accumulated. The caterer got there about an hour early to set up the food tables. It was almost time for the dance to start. Would people brave the snow to come to the aid of a needy alcoholic?

The dance was supposed to start at 7:00 PM. By 7:15 no one had shown up. By 7:30 a handful of people had shown up. Then a miracle happened. Buses started pulling in from the surrounding areas. One nursing home sent a bus; several high schools sent busloads of teenagers. Other treatment centers sent van loads of patients, and the local churches sent a couple of buses. When it was all over, they had made several thousand dollars on admission tickets alone.

Ms. Towers went to Arkansas. At the writing of this story, she has maintained a year of sobriety. The surplus money from the fund-raiser went into a memorial fund named after the woman who died in jail. The area treatment centers jointly sponsor a fund-raiser every year to raise funds for indigent chemical dependence health care. The funds are used to cover health care for those without insurance coverage. Some care is provided locally. Some patients are sent to Arkansas like Ms. Towers had been.

If this sounds like a fairy tale, perhaps it is. Like all such tales, its intent is to precipitate introspective thought. Hopefully, such questions as

"Why?" "Why not?" and "Why can't we do what Arkansas does?" will be contemplated. More importantly perhaps the question, "Why does chemical dependence inpatient treatment often cost $1000 a day or more?" will be considered. Why, indeed.

UNIT THREE

EARLY RECOVERY

Chapter X

THE HOLY SALSA ORDEAL

Skip sighed as he lifted his empty suitcase down from the closet. He remembered when he'd first come here. God, how he'd wanted to split. But something had kept him here. The real irony was that now that he was being discharged, he wasn't sure he really wanted to go. Wayne, his AA sponsor, had told him that not wanting to leave treatment and being scared that he couldn't stay sober were normal, healthy reactions to being discharged from treatment.

He methodically emptied all the dresser drawers. Now he was ready to tackle the night stand next to his bed. What an assortment of odds and ends . Here was his desire chip they'd given it to him at his first AA meeting. Some old timer had told him to put it in his mouth when he wanted a drink and when it dissolved, it'd be OK for him to have that drink. Of course, the chip wasn't made to dissolve. That was the point . It would never be OK for him to take another drink, no matter how badly he wanted it. Another old timer had told him that "one drink would be too many and a thousand would never be enough." Somehow, he found that amusing irony comforting.

He must have already fingered the "Serenity Prayer" that was printed on the chip almost a thousand times now whenever he felt stressed He smiled as he slipped the chip into his pocket. He couldn't imagine leaving it behind. He continued rummaging through the drawer. There were a couple of business cards He'd got those from several people at AA meetings. They all had home phone numbers written on their backs. They'd all said not to hesitate to call if he ever needed to or if he just wanted to talk. Surprisingly, it hadn't been that hard. He'd better pack these so he could keep the phone numbers.

He found a piece of paper and turned it over. It looked official. It had his name and hospital number addressographed across the top. He'd better check it before he threw it away. It turned out to be his copy of his informed consent for his taking Antabuse. At first he'd been just a little leery of taking it. Then Wayne helped him realize that taking Antabuse was a way of taking AA's first step every day. It meant he had to own being powerless over alcohol every time he took the medicine. It also meant turning his will to drink over to his Higher Power every time he took it.

Skip stopped packing and sat down for a minute. What was it the nurse had said before she had him sign this form? She'd explained that Antabuse (Disulfiram) blocks how alcohol is metabolized in the body so that a strong reaction occurs if alcohol enters the body.[1] She explained that was why a person who took Antabuse had to avoid all forms of alcohol, external as well as internal. Both forms would cause a toxic reaction for someone who had Antabuse in his or her system. She'd described the toxic reaction in great detail, and she'd made him repeat it before she had him sign the form. He'd really memorized them. He could still list the reaction symptoms: flushing, increased blood pressure, difficulty breathing, and the possibility of pain in or around the area of his heart accompanied by severe vomiting.[2]

Skip glanced down at his hands. He'd clenched his right hand into a fist. He was more anxious than he'd realized about this Antabuse stuff. He had to admit the reactions sounded pretty terrifying. That's why he was taking it. He needed to be scared of it so he wouldn't drink again. He couldn't afford to because his doctor had told him he'd die if he did. He'd had a bad case of pancreatitis this last time. He couldn't risk another flare up. He couldn't drink again. At least for right now, his life depended on him taking Antabuse.

Two weeks later, Skip was at home waking up in his own bed. He'd been out of the hospital for a couple of weeks now. He'd spent the first week going to meetings almost around the clock. He'd gone back to work the second week. He wasn't as scared about staying sober as he had been because so far it hadn't been a problem. He hadn't wanted a drink for several days now. When he'd asked Wayne about this, he'd told him it was because he was working the AA program on a daily basis.

A fleeting frown crossed his face. Last night Mary had told him that she and the kids were feeling left out of his new life. It was true he was spending almost every waking hour either at work or at a meeting. He was going to make it up to them today though. After going out for breakfast, they were going on a family outing to the zoo. It'd been years since he'd gone to the zoo with them. Zeke had been just a toddler then, and Amanda hadn't even been born yet.

---

[1] Burkhalter, P.K. (1975) Nursing Care of the Alcoholic and Drug Abuser. New York: McGraw-Hill.
[2] Ibid.

That trip hadn't turned out well. He'd got drunk and fought with Mary. She and Zeke had taken a cab home and left him at the zoo. He still remembered how stranded and let down he'd felt He'd dealt with his feelings by leaving in a drunken rage. He'd felt really macho when he'd peeled out of the parking lot in the family pickup. He ended up totaling the family truck. He'd been lucky he wasn't badly hurt. Today was going to be different. It was going to be special. He planned on undoing some of the pain it caused in the past.

* * * * *

The restaurant they were at was crowded and somewhat noisy, so they ate outside on the patio. Mary was sipping her coffee while she helped Amanda "mash up" her fried eggs so they looked like scrambled eggs. It felt good being outdoors in the fresh spring air. He spooned some of the salsa onto his eggs. It was particularly good here. The restaurant made it themselves with chunks of fresh tomatoes, jalepenos and onions. Then he passed the salsa onto Mary. Judging by the smile on her face, she was enjoying herself. She'd been keeping up a constant line of chatter interspersing it sporadically with bursts of childlike giggles. Her giggles were music to his ears. He hadn't seen her this happy in years.

He'd just reached for a second tortilla when he noticed that he felt a little odd. Mary was staring at him. He jokingly asked her, "What's wrong honey? You look like you've seen a ghost."

She thought for a moment before replying, "Not a ghost. It's you. Your face has got real red all of the sudden. It looks almost sunburned. We've only been out here a few minutes, and we're in the shade."

It was then that he suddenly figured out what was happening. He was having trouble breathing, and his throat felt tight. He tried to stay calm. "Mary, I want you to take the kids to the car. I'll pay for this, and then I want you to drive me to the emergency room."

A look of alarm crossed Mary's face. Seeing it, Skip continued, "There's no cause for alarm. I'm just having an Antabuse reaction. They told me if it happened that I needed to get medical attention. Stay calm. I'll meet you at the car."

* * * * *

Several hours later the ordeal was over. He was beginning to relax. They'd treated him at the ER and released him. He'd been confused about what triggered the Antabuse reaction until the ER doctor told him that some local Mexican restaurants put a touch of beer in the salsa. They left the salsa sitting out on the tables, and the beer kept the salsa from spoiling. Evidently, he'd ingested enough beer to cause the Antabuse reaction when he'd eaten the salsa earlier. He'd called Wayne from the ER. Wayne drove over to be with Skip. He told him that now he knew what to expect if he drank again. Then he made a point of stressing that the reaction would be much worse though because he'd only had a tiny amount of alcohol in his system today.

Seeing the discouraged look on Skip's face, Wayne continued. "You know Skip, this will all get easier in time. You aren't going to have to be on Antabuse forever. Judging by how you're working the program, following the steps, and going to meetings, I'd bet money you can stop taking Antabuse within a year. But you can't rush it. Only you will know when you feel ready to take the daily 'first step' without Antabuse to back it up."

Skip smiled briefly. Wayne looked at him quizzically, "OK, what else is going on in that head of yours?"

Skip thought a moment before answering. "I'm just thinking about how I've let my wife and kids down again. I really blew it the last time we went to the zoo. I got drunk and fought with Mary. She took Zeke and left me in a cab. I got mad and took off in the truck. I ended up totaling it. I'd wanted to make up for it today. What happens? I make a mess of it again."

Wayne looked at Skip and shook his head in disagreement. "Skip, you didn't intentionally mess up today. It's not like you knew the salsa had beer in it. Don't you think your wife can see the difference between why this zoo trip fell through and why the last one was ruined? Cut her some slack! Better yet, cut yourself some. Comprende?"

Skip answered, "Yeah, I guess so. You're always telling me all I can really change in this world is my own behavior and attitudes...that I can't change other people, places, or things. Maybe this is one time when I need to focus on changing my attitude. It's a cinch I can't change what happened today. You're right. I can stop blaming myself."

* * * * *

Later that evening he was sitting out on the back deck with Mary after they'd put the kids to bed. He knew he'd never find a better time to talk to her about what had happened today. "Mary, I'm really sorry about what happened today. I'd wanted it to be really special."

Mary looked at him. Then she said, "I know. What happened wasn't your fault."

Skip put his arm around Mary's shoulders. "It meant so much to me to have you there with me today. I love you so much it hurts sometimes."

Mary tilted her chin up, and Skip leaned down and kissed her. Wayne was always telling him there was a spiritual lesson in everything that happened and that our Higher Power never sends us anything we can't handle. Maybe he was right. Maybe there was a reason today happened the way it did. Right now he was just grateful to be standing there looking at the stars with the woman he loved.

Chapter XI

BABY STEPS

Becky opened her eyes. Wide. Her room was still here. It looked like it had the night before when she'd drifted off to sleep. Things seemed the same, her dream had seemed so real. She'd been in a bar with her friends. She could still feel the pleasant warmth of the scotch's relaxation spreading through her body. Laughter had been so easy, her dancing effortless. She'd let her friends refill her glass again and again. Abruptly the dream's tone had changed. Suddenly she caught her reflection in the dance floor mirror. She was barely able to stand up straight. Her makeup was smeared, and her hair was in disarray. People were staring at her, pointing and laughing. She'd lifted her glass to her mouth and missed. To her horror, she watched big blotches of the wet alcohol laden liquid cascade down the front of her party dress. Everyone laughed louder, harder. She wanted to dig a hole and crawl in to get away from their spiteful laughing. Instead, she dropped the glass. It shattered into thousands of tiny shreds before her eyes. The next thing she knew she was listening to her dog barking. The sound brought her awake. Here she was in her room. Awake, and sober.

The dream had been so real that she actually felt guilty. She'd fought hard for these eleven months of sobriety. Thanks to the dream she almost felt like she'd relapsed and thrown it all away in a few foolish moments of self destruction. They'd told her at the AA meetings that this would happen. They'd said she'd have dreams of drinking that were so real she'd feel guilty and swear she was having a hangover.

Slowly she sat up and took a deep breath. What a way to start her day! She automatically slipped into the habit Anita, her sponsor, had taught her. Anita had called it the "daily please and thank you."

"Please, God," Becky thought, "just for today, let me be sober."

She felt an immediate sense of relief. She no longer felt the dream's residue of panic. She was grateful it had only been a dream. She'd have to call Anita and tell her about it as soon as she was awake enough to be coherent.

She finished her shower, dressed, and grabbed a donut for breakfast. Then she put on her makeup. The stark reality of the dream had already faded. She'd probably over-reacted to it. She'd better hurry or she'd be late for work. She'd call Anita later on today when she had time after she got home from work. Right now she couldn't take the time.

As Becky backed out of her driveway, she began thinking about all the meetings she'd attended. She'd done the ninety meetings in ninety days her treatment counselor had advised when she'd left the hospital. She was going to fewer meetings now. She no longer felt the desperate urgency to "get to a meeting" that she had in the beginning. It was easier to believe she was going to stay sober so she wasn't anxious about it. She was surprised the dream had affected her the way it did.

Actually, she was beginning to question the wisdom of fostering dependence on all those meetings. At times she saw the whole AA program as a bunch of fanatical, overly strict discipline. It was getting less and less important to turn things over to a Higher Power. She'd tried unsuccessfully to talk to Anita about her ambivalence several times. She was afraid to be honest about her doubts and concerns. She'd even discussed the program's prescribed dependence on meetings and a Higher Power as just another symptom of her co-dependence with her therapist. He'd agreed that perhaps she should focus instead on promoting her own independence.

She braked to miss a car that had pulled out in front of her. She was almost to work. Maybe the dream was connected to the step work she'd been doing. Anita had helped her work through the first two steps. Now she was focusing her attention on taking the third step. She kept feeling like she was slipping in and out of the third step. It really brought out her ambivalence, and she was stuck. She couldn't go forward, and she couldn't go back. It was all connected with her dependence/independence conflicts. Anita kept telling her that turning your will and your life over to the care of a Higher Power was a way to assert independence. Becky kept questioning how giving your power away by turning it over to something outside yourself could foster independence.

Anita had explained that turning things over allowed that outside power greater than yourself to integrate into your soul and into your very sense of being or of self. It literally became a part of you. She said that resulted in an inner sense, a knowing of absolute power and serenity. Becky had told her that it all sounded like a bunch of double talk.

Anita tried a new approach. "Becky, turning your will and your life over to a Higher Power on a daily basis is just like turning on a light switch.

Turning it on allows a surge of energy to flow through us and empower us to create a better reality."

Anita could tell by the expression on Becky's face that she wasn't really understanding what she was saying. She decided to let the topic of "Higher Power/Inner Power" go until another opportunity to discuss it arose. As an after thought she'd told Becky to read the Big Book's promises.[1] She'd explained that they gave a full description of what happened when you became empowered by your Higher Power.

Becky turned into the parking lot at work and pulled into a parking space that had opened up near the hospital entrance. She was being silly getting hung up on this third step. She hardly ever thought anymore about having a drink. That had to mean she was better. Working with her therapist should be enough. If she stayed in therapy, she probably wouldn't need to take all 12 of AA's "blessed" steps anyway.

Then she remembered the dream. It had seemed so real at the time. Maybe it had been trying to tell her she could handle social drinking now that she'd been sober for so long. Face it, the first part of her dream had been fun. She hadn't had that much fun since she stopped drinking. She couldn't forget the latter part of the dream either. It had seemed as real, and it had been extremely unpleasant. She couldn't go back to being a hopeless, out-of-control drunk that everyone laughed at behind her back and to her face. Enough. She had to get her mind on work and her patients now. It was time she quit obsessing about all this stuff.

* * * * *

Becky was sitting at the nurse's station. There was a half-drunk cup of coffee sitting on the deck in front of her. She'd just hung up from speaking to the lab when the phone rang again. The switchboard operator said there was a man on the line who claimed to be an old friend of hers. He was insisting on talking to her, and the operator was checking with Becky to see if it was OK to put the call through. Becky told her to put him through.

When the call came through, Becky said. "Hello, this is Ms. Walters on 2-North. May I help you?"

---

[1] Alcoholics Anonymous (1976) Alcoholics Anonymous: The Story of How Many Thousands of Men and Women Have Recovered from Alcohol. Third Edition, New York: Alcoholics Anonymous World Services, Inc., pp. 83-84.

There was a moment of silence on the other end before a friendly, masculine voice spoke. "Becky, this is Ed. Thank goodness they put me through. My plane just got in town. My meeting isn't until tomorrow morning. I was hoping we could get together for a few drinks. I've got this 'command performance' party that a client's throwing. I thought you'd enjoy going to the party with me. What do you say?"

Becky was surprised to hear Ed's voice. They hadn't talked in months. He didn't know about her recovery or that she considered herself an alcoholic. She wanted to see him anyway. He was fun, and she'd been bored lately. They'd had lots of fun partying and drinking together over the years.

She finally said, "Ed! What a delightful surprise! It would be wonderful to see you. What time's your party?"

Ed responded, "It starts around eight. Nobody will get there until at least 10:00 PM. At least nobody that matters. We could make a night of it, what do you say?"

OK. I would like to have dinner first before we go to the party. Do you think we could get together over dinner rather than over a few drinks?"

"Sure. Anything you say. Why don't you meet me at the Carlisle in about an hour? That'll give us time to grab a bite to eat. Then we can go by your place so you can get into your party clothes. We'll stop by my hotel on the way to the party so I can get into my tux. Do you have something formal to slip into on such short notice?"

"Going places with you was always a challenge, Ed. I'll see what I can do. I'll leave work in about forty five minutes. I'll take a cab from my place to the Carlisle so we won't be having to drive two cars all over town. Thanks for the invite. Later. "Bye."

Becky glanced at her watch as she hung up the phone. She barely had time to make it home, shower and do her hair. She'd just have to wait until tomorrow to call Anita and talk to her about the dream. She really needed this night out on the town, and if she called Anita before she went she might tell her not to go. Most of the AA old timers kept advising everyone to "change playmates and playthings." When she'd asked Anita to explain, Anita had said, "That means to stay away from bars and old drinking buddies. They make it too easy to start drinking again." That's why she felt sure Anita would tell her not to go out on the town with Ed.

* * * * *

The lighting in the restaurant was subdued. Once they were seated, things went smoothly until the waiter came to take their orders for drinks. Ed ordered his usual and was halfway through ordering a scotch and water for Becky before she stopped him.

"That's all right. I don't want a drink. I'm dieting. Bring me a mineral water with a twist of lime, please." As the waiter turned to go, Becky noticed Ed looking at her a little strangely. "Well," she said, "spit it out. Something is obviously bothering you."

Ed cleared his throat. He seemed uncomfortable with what he was about to say. "I don't know just how to put this, but I never thought I'd see the day when you turned down a scotch and water. What gives?"

She laughed and answered. "Didn't you hear? I'm dieting. Besides I'd rather catch up on what's been happening to you than drink myself into oblivion. Mona told me you went on an extended sailing jaunt last summer. I want to hear all about it."

Her ploy worked. Ed started talking about sailing and forgot all about Becky's not drinking.

Later, they were out on the dance floor. Becky felt awkward dancing with him initially. She didn't remember it being this way dancing with Ed....or with anyone, for that matter. She suddenly realized that in the past she'd used the alcohol to loosen her up and to make dancing easier. It had blunted her self-consciousness. Now she missed the old, relaxed, easy dancing. It would be so easy to ask Ed to buy her a drink. She'd just drink one to take the edge off.

Ed noticed Becky's stiffness. He'd never seen her this way before. "What's wrong, Becky? You don't seem quite yourself."

She smiled nervously and replied, "It must have been something I ate. I don't feel well. I think I'll try going to the ladies room. I'll only be a moment." Ed excused her and she headed for the restroom.

She was halfway across the dance floor before she realized she'd be walking right by the bar. In this crowd she could grab a drink and down it without Ed even knowing . She reached into her bag for some money and approached the bar. She forced herself to smile as she called the bartender over to her. He asked her what
she wanted to drink.

This was it. She either bought the drink and drank it or she didn't. She had a choice. Boy, talk about standing at the crossroads. She wanted the drink so badly. But she didn't want to throw away her eleven months of sobriety either. One drink surely wouldn't hurt. Nobody's have to know, and she'd enjoy her time with Ed so much more if she could relax a little bit.

The bartender interrupted, "Well, Miss. What will it be? I haven't got all night!"

He must be getting impatient with her indecision. She handed him the bill that was in her hand. "Pardon me," she said, "would you change this for me, please. I need to make a phone call."

He gave her the change. She took it and walked on to the restroom. Just outside its door there was a telephone. She stopped and dialed Anita's number. As the phone was ringing, Becky realized she was taking the third step for real this time. When she'd decided to call Anita rather than buying that drink, she'd turned her will and her life over to the power of the AA program and her sponsor.

Anita answered the phone. Beck's voice cracked as she said, "Anita, this is Becky. I'm in a mess. I'm at a club on a date with an old boy friend. Things are pretty tense because I'm not drinking. He can tell something's wrong....that I'm not relaxed, and that I'm not dancing like I used to and that I'm anxious. I want a drink so badly that I walked up to the bar to order a drink. Finally I got some change instead so I could call you."

Anita instantly replied. "Where are you?" When Becky told her, Anita said, "I want you to go into the ladies' room. They've got a sofa you can sit on until I get there. It'll only take me 10-15 minutes to get there. Keep saying the Serenity Prayer over and over to yourself. Don't worry about your boyfriend. He'll be OK. It's important that you stay in the restroom. You'll be less tempted to drink. We'll explain things to your boyfriend after I get there."

Becky agreed and hung up the phone. She walked into the restroom and over to the sofa and sat down. She turned her head to the side and noticed little roses running up and down the wall paper. Then she turned her head back and looked straight ahead into the mirror that was across the room. There was no one else in the restroom, and when she looked closely at her reflection she noticed her lips were moving. She made it through the prayer whispering the first time. Then, since she was still alone, she said the words out loud: "God, grant me the serenity to accept things I cannot change, courage to change the things I can, and wisdom to know the difference. Thy will, not mine, be done.[2]

[2] Alcoholics Anonymous (1952) Twelve Steps and Twelve Traditions. New York: Alcoholics Anonymous World Services, Inc., p. 41.

UNIT FOUR

SPECIAL SITUATIONS

Chapter XII

PLANTING SEEDS

Juan had been in the hospital for three long days. He was coming off heroin. He felt like death warmed over. He couldn't handle all the rules they had in this place. They were even telling him he couldn't smoke in the hospital. He'd been smoking since he turned 13 three years ago. These jerks were treating him like he was still a kid.

He knew more about survival than these jerks could imagine in their wildest dreams. He'd made a bad mistake when he went home and asked his Mom for money. At first, he thought she was going to give it to him. She and her old man told him they were going to the bank. Instead, they brought him to this joint. What a fool he'd been to trust them.

He'd got to the point last night where he had to have a cigarette. So he went into his bathroom and lit up. The psychiatric tech that was making rounds had caught him. They searched his room, confiscated his cigarettes, and put him on room restriction. When his doctor had come in this morning to make rounds he'd reminded him that putting him on room restriction was a violation of his patients' rights if it wasn't done to protect him from harming himself or others. He'd read that on the wall where they had the rights posted. Anyway, he'd got his doctor to take him off room restriction. Now it was only a matter of time before he blew this joint. All he had to do was wait for the right moment.

He waited until the psychiatric tech was busy with some other patients and the nurses and doctors were meeting in a conference room. The other psychiatric tech was on break. The "locked doors" on this unit were a piece of cake. You didn't even need a credit card to get them open. All you had to do was push then just right. He needed a fix, and he wasn't staying around here anymore. Screw them, he was out of here.

When the psychiatric tech had discovered Juan was missing, the nurse called his doctor, his mother, and the administrator on call. Then she'd called the police and filed a missing person's report. Juan must have left about 9:30 AM. By 5:30 PM the police had apprehended him. The police took him back to the station. Juan was stuck there while the police decided what to do with him.

Juan was old enough that they couldn't take him to the hospital against his will. It looked like he was going to have to stay in police custody until his mother came and got him. He'd attacked one of the policemen that had apprehended him, so they were unwilling to release him. When they called his mother, she'd said she was unwilling to post bail and pick him up unless he was willing to return to the hospital. So far, the kid refused to go back.

* * * * *

Juan awoke to the sound of his cell door opening. The guard told him there was a juvenile worker here to talk to him. Juan went with the guard. He tried to ignore the obscenities yelled at them as they passed. He'd been treated like a sex object on the streets sometimes. He only let that happen when he needed to work a John to score his next fix. This was different. He wasn't in control. He wasn't calling the shots.

Juan expected the juvenile worker to be some prissy-assed "Miss Goody-Two Shoes" that didn't know her ass from a hole in the ground. When they got to the visitor's room, all he could see was this ex-Marine type standing with his back turned while he stared out the window. The man had on a pair of faded jeans, a white tee shirt, and sneakers. His left sleeve was rolled up. He had a pack of cigarettes tucked into the rolled up sleeve. For a second, Juan thought he'd time tripped back to the fifties. This man looked just like the pictures he'd seen of what was considered cool over forty years ago. He even had tattoos all over his biceps. This sure wasn't what he'd expected.

Slowly the man turned. He stared straight into Juan's eyes, pulled a chair out from the table, and propped one leg up on it. He pulled his cigarettes out of his sleeve, fished a box of matches out of his pocket, got one out of the box, and stooped to light the match on the bottom of his shoe. He inhaled as he lit the cigarette. Then he slowly blew smoke directly into Juan's face as he said "Sit down, punk."

Somehow, Juan didn't feel like arguing. He sat down. He didn't break eye contact with the man. There was something about him and his stare that didn't encourage inattention. The man took another drag off his cigarette. This time he exhaled the smoke over Juan's left shoulder.

"Listen up, kid. You've got one chance to get out of here. You attacked a police officer last might. They'd just as soon turn you over to this bunch they keep locked up in here. They think it'd teach you a lesson. Your Mom has washed her hands of you. The hospital doesn't want you back. If I was you, I'd start listening real close."

Juan glared back at the man. The dude had an attitude problem. He'd have to fix it for him. "Hey, man, no offense, but I'm a juvenile. I can't stay in jail. Besides, it's over-crowded in here. They don't have room for characters like me whose only mistake was fighting back when being wrongfully apprehended. I committed no crime. What I did was self-defense. You can't scare me with your threats. Let me get before a judge, and I'll be out of here in a red hot minute."

The man laughed. Then he blew smoke in Juan's face again. "You cocky bastard, when are you going to get it through that thick little skull of yours that the game is up? They'd dredged up your record. There's a warrant out on you for some major shoplifting. You're facing a felony. You'll be tried as an adult, you get treated like an adult. There are some inmates in this joint who'd love to introduce you to an entirely new meaning of the term 'adult treatment' Comprende?"

Juan definitely didn't like the turn this conversation was taking. He needed some time to think, so he asked the man for a cigarette. Juan's eyes wandered over the room as he savored his first drag. He started to take another when the man told him to quit stalling. So, he looked the man in the eye and said. "You said I had one way out of here. What gives?"

The man actually smiled as he answered. "I thought you might want to hear some more about that. I run this new drug treatment center for juvenile cases. Most of the cases are street punks like yourself. I'm here to invite you to come join us. Trust me, it's no piece of cake. It'll be a challenge for you. If you meet it head on, you have a chance at getting a life back for yourself. You'll agree to having no visitors, no television, no radio, and very little free time. You'll be busy in confronting group sessions as well as heavy duty one-on-one sessions with a counselor who's as street-wise as you. He's light years ahead of you because he'd been where you are now. He'd had 10 years of being drug free since then to sharpen his wits."

The man paused to light another cigarette before continuing. "You'll be allowed one phone call a week to your mother. She'll come to the family sessions one a week after you've been in my place for three weeks. Altogether, you're looking at about 12 weeks of hard work. If you come through it and don't mess up and end up back in this place, you'll have a real life to look forward to again. You won't have to steal or put out any more to support your habit. You don't look like the type that enjoys going down on faggots anyway."

Juan clenched his fists. This dude was getting under his skin. He'd better let him keep talking though because it sounded like this dude had his ticket out of here.

The man continued. "Chill out. I didn't say you were a faggot. Give me a break. Anyway, as I was saying, we understand what it's like to live on the streets and support a habit. We've been there, and we got out. We know the way out, and we're willing to teach it to you. You'll find out we know how to get your attention and get you to listen. The choice is yours. By the way, I'm known as 'Doc'. If you decide to take this challenge, they'll know where to find me. One other thing, kid, you've only got the next four hours to decide because that's when the judge will be seeing us in court."

Doc stubbed his cigarette out in the ashtray, got up, turned and left the room. Juan took a deep breath. He was really in a mess this time. He barely had time to stand up before the guard walked over to escort him back to his cell.

* * * * *

That had been almost two months ago. Juan had ended up choosing to come to Doc's place. It'd been pretty rough at first, but he'd got used to it. He'd actually even made some friends in this place. Tonight was family therapy night. Juan had been wondering what he'd say to his Mom all day. A few minutes later, he found himself following Mike into the big group room. There must be twenty families represented in the room. He searched the sea of faces for his Mom's face. It took a while for him to spot her, but he finally found her on the fifth row back, three chairs from the left. She smiled at him as she caught his eye. They'd get to visit after the therapy session was over.

The room got quiet. Doc had entered the room and walked up to the podium to welcome everyone. He explained how the group worked.

"There are three chairs up front. One is for me, the other for the chosen patient, and the other for that patient's significant other. When you sit in these chairs, you can say anything you want to each other. The whole purpose is for you to open up and communicate feelings to each other. The rules are you have to be honest. People in the audience could offer feedback to the two sitting in the chairs if they raised their hand and waited to be called upon. I call this technique the 'family hot seat'. It's been quite effective over the years. It can be scary, but here's where family's learn to fight fair and to show love. The payoffs of love and honest communication are worth the price. Remember, it's healthy to be scared when you first try something like this. I'll be here to see that everything stays safe and under control."

After he finished talking, he quietly looked around the room. Juan's pulse was racing. He and his Mom hadn't done this hot seat thing yet. He was afraid they'd get their chance tonight. He'd started opening up about his feelings in his therapy sessions and in groups. He wasn't sure he was ready to do so with his mom in front of all these people. To his horror, he heard Doc say, "Juan, why don't you and your Mom come and be first." Juan grimaced and stood up before he and his Mom walked toward the chairs.

Juan knew from sitting through these sessions before that it was up to him to start things off. He forced himself to fight his nervousness and say, "Hi, Mom. Glad you could come. Why don't you introduce yourself."

It was forever before his Mom responded. "Hi, Juan. I'm glad to be here. My name is Barbara, and I'm glad to meet everyone." Then the silence began.

Juan couldn't decide what to do. What should he say to his mother?

God knows, they hadn't really talked since he'd left home. Before he'd left, all she'd done was fight with his father and nag at him to do his chores. His therapist had been trying to get him to remember what had happened when he was a child. He'd remembered hiding in the closet to keep away from his father's drunken rages. He also remembered his mother lying hurt and bleeding on the floor.

He'd remembered the nights when his father never came home at all. Those had been the nights when his mother spent time with him. She'd get up periodically to walk over and look out the window, but he still had her all to himself. She must have been worried about his father. He could tell she was afraid of him at the same time. With all that going on, how had she had any love left over for him? The funny thing was, when he was little, she'd had lots of love for him. She'd always been hugging him and telling him how much she loved him. When had it ended?

He couldn't remember feeling like his mother loved him since he'd started hanging out with the neighborhood gang. Suddenly, his attention was called back to the crowded room. His mother had broken the silence by clearing her throat. Then she said. "Juan, I've been seeing Doc in individual sessions. He thinks its important for us to talk about how it was when you were a little boy. You were always a good little boy. No matter how bad things got around the house, you were always there to try to put the pieces back together. When you got older and started hanging out with the gang, it was never the same again. You started being hateful and resentful. You never had anything nice to say."

Juan felt everyone's attention focus on him. He had to say something. He swallowed hard before beginning, "Well, Mom....it's like this. I finally just gave up on the mess at home. I couldn't live like that anymore. I had to get away from Dad's drunken rages and the way you always made excuses for him. I had to make a life for myself. It was easier surviving on the streets than it was at home. After Dad threatened to kill me if I stood up to him again it just seemed safer to stay away."

His mother sighed and stared at her hands as she clenched and unclenched them in her lap. Then she looked up at him.

"Juan, it won't be like that anymore. I've sworn out a peace warrant against him. He can't come near you or me or he'll be arrested. I'm living with another man now. Henry is a nice man. I've got a job. With my money and the money Henry makes on his job, we can afford to have you live with us. I want you at home. I want it to be the way it used to between us."

Barbara paused, then in a shaky voice she said, "However, if you come live with us, there are some things you need to agree to before you come. There will be no drinking or drugging in the house by you or your friends. I don't want you drinking or drugging, period. You'll have to have periodic random drug screens done. You'll have to pull your load around the house, and you'll have to finish school."

Juan was puzzled. Maybe he'd been here too long, but it almost seemed as if his Mom was scared to face him. She'd sounded unsure of herself when she explained the "rules and conditions" of him coming home to live. How could he jump on her case for nagging him when she sounded so vulnerable? She hadn't sounded demanding or like she was nagging him. She'd just made a simple, matter-of-fact statement about the way things would have to be.

She'd even seemed genuinely eager to have him come home. What would it be like without his father there? What would it be like with this Henry character in the house? Did he dare give it a chance? He glanced towards his mother before answering.

"Mom, I don't know. It all sounds OK, but how can I trust that things will really be OK between us or that Dad will stay away from us. How can I know whether or not Henry and I can get along? I want to come home. I want to stay clean. I want to 'pull my load'. I've got to take some time to think about this and to figure out if I can trust what you said."

Doc shifted in his chair. Juan knew that was his signal that he was about to say something. Doc had been looking back and forth between him and his mother. Finally, Doc said, "I want you both to realize you just communicated with each other as adults. You were honest, and you weren't playing games. You've made progress."

Then he focused on Barbara before saying, "I think Juan will be ready to come home in about two weeks. He needs that time to think about your offer. He also needs to work on trust issues in some joint sessions with you and me. He may decide not to come home. That's his choice. You'll need to accept him and to support his drug free lifestyle regardless of what he decides."

Then Doc turned toward Juan. "You'll need to be completely honest with yourself and us in the joint sessions we'll be having. You may or may not come to trust her again. You'll need to work at maintaining open communication with her after you leave regardless of where you decide to live. This had been a good start for the two of you. Why don't you both return to your seats in the audience, let's give another family a turn at this."

* * * * *

Somehow, Juan got through those last two weeks. Mary Alice, the young nurse that worked the day shift at the center, had been working with him a lot on what she called "discharge planning". When she'd first approached him about it, he thought she was crazy for spending so much time about what it was going to be like when he left and what he needed to do to stay clean. Now he wondered. The closer his discharge date came, the less he wanted to leave.

Mary Alice had spent time with him figuring out ways he could stay busy without hanging around his old friends or hangouts. What she'd said made sense. It's be a lot easier to stay clean if he wasn't around drugs or people who used them. He'd been worried about where he was going to stay after he left. He'd finally decided to go along with his mother's conditions and live at home. He couldn't just sit around in his bedroom all the time. That'd drive him crazy, big time. Mary Alice had said he'd need to fill his time up with meetings, and she offered to get him a ride to a Narcotics Anonymous (NA) meeting in his neighborhood.

Juan went to that NA meeting before he was discharged so he could see what it was like. He was surprised to see several guys there from the streets. One told "his story" during the meeting. Juan had identified with almost every word that came out of his mouth. The dude had introduced himself as "CQ". Mary Alice let him stay after the meeting to talk to CQ. He'd ended up asking him to be his sponsor. CQ agreed. The two of them had been busy planning ways he could stay busy after he was discharged so he could stay clean. Of course, he'd be going back to the center for after care and continue going to meetings.

He'd also made a verbal contract with Mary Alice to call Doc's center or CQ any time he needed to talk or felt like using. He'd asked her for her phone number and she'd refused to give it to him. She'd said to do so would be unprofessional. She'd explained she was his nurse, not a social acquaintance or friend. She'd said if he called the center and talked to anyone who was available he wouldn't become too dependent on any one person. He had to admit that made sense.

Actually, the way he and CQ had hit it off, he probably wouldn't have to be calling the staff at the center that much anyway. He wasn't nearly as worried about leaving now that he had him for a sponsor. CQ understood what he'd gone through. He understood what he was going through now. Thankfully he'd promised to be there to help him through whatever he encountered in the future.

Juan's attention was yanked away from his thoughts when he heard his name called out. He'd been sitting on the stage as a member of the "graduating class". He stood up, looked around the room and slowly walked to the front. He reached out his hand to accept the mug Doc was handing him. On one side the mug read, "I graduated from Doc's place." On the other side the mug read, "One Day at a Time". Doc hugged him after he handed him the mug.

After the ceremony was over, Juan walked around the room shaking hands, saying good-byes, and hugging people who were there. CQ had come with a bunch of the guys from his "home meeting" (the NA meeting he and CQ always went to come hell or high water). The last person he hugged was Mary Alice. Smiling at her, he said. "Thanks for giving me my life back." As he backed off from the hug, he noticed tears in her eyes. She quietly said, "You did all the work. We just planted the seeds."

Chapter XIII

THE DOCTOR MADE ME DO IT

Mrs. Perkins hung up the phone with a sigh. Her dog lifted his head up off his paws to glance at her quizzically. She slowly walked to the door. She was looking out the screen door, but her expression made it clear that her mind was a thousand miles away. The tea kettle must have been whistling for almost a full minute before it caught her attention and she turned and made her way to the kitchen. She grimaced with every step; her arthritis was really acting up today. But that wasn't why she'd just called her doctor. She'd called him because her back was hurting her again. It had just never been the same after the surgery. It had been months now since her surgery and none of the PT or pain pills he'd put her on had seemed to help. The muscle relaxers helped somewhat, but she wondered if what they really did was adjust her mind so she just didn't care any more.

The pain was so sudden and sharp when she reached for the tea kettle that she had to grip the stove top for support. She couldn't go on like this. She'd been to two other doctors, and they'd both prescribed something different for her. She'd found that she could sleep at night if she took one pill from each prescription at the same time. She knew that might be dangerous, so she'd only been doing it at bedtime. It was beginning to look as if she'd have to start trying that during her waking hours too if she was going to get any relief. She'd just talked to her surgeon, and he'd refused to order a refill for her. Now she'd have to find another doctor to get the pain pills he'd been ordering for her or else she wouldn't have the third type of pill she needed. The last thing she felt like was getting out of the house. Besides that, it was impossible for her to drive. She couldn't ask Betty Low, her daughter, to take her because she didn't want to be a burden. She didn't want her family to know how many pills she was having to take just to make it through the day. She'd have to call a cab, but first she had to find a doctor who could see her today.

That night Mrs. Perkiness felt exhausted. It had been all she could to make it to the doctor's office, sit for hours in the waiting room, answer the doctor's questions, get her prescription, take the cab to the pharmacy, wait to get her prescription filled, and take the cab home. Of course, the cab with all that driving and waiting had cost a fortune. But it had been worth it, he'd ordered the medication she wanted with three refills. It'd be a while before she had to repeat today's performance. She'd taken all three of her pills, but sleep still eluded her. Here it was almost 2:00 AM and she was still wide awake. Her pain, although better, was still constant. She flipped on the television. That gave her an idea. When John had been alive the two of them always had a nightcap before going to bed. She hadn't tried that for years, but anything was worth a try so she could get to sleep and escape this constant pain.

Several weeks later, on her eighty third birthday, Mrs. Perkins found herself taking all three pills every four hours around the clock. She usually had to have a scotch and water between doses to get rid of the pain. She had a maid who came in and cleaned once a week. The last time she'd come, she'd made a big deal about all the medication that Mrs. Perkins was taking. Can you believe it? The woman had the audacity to criticize her for taking her medication! She'd gone on and on about how it was dangerous to mix pain medication with tranquilizers. Bessie thought she knew all there was to know about medicine just because she'd gone to nursing school for less than a year when she was a girl. She'd got married and they'd kicked her out of the nursing school, so she'd never really graduated. But you'd never know it to hear her hand out advice the way she did. Still and all, Bessie was a good maid. You just had to tune out her busybody intrusions here and there.

That afternoon, she'd just taken her mid-afternoon double scotch when the doorbell rang. She peeked out the window from behind the curtain to see who was at the door. To her dismay, she recognized Pastor Edwards from her church. She managed to yell, "just a minute..." as she reached for the breath mints she kept in the desk drawer. What luck, here she'd just had a drink and her minister was at the door. She'd just have to put on a good front. At least the pain was momentarily under control.

She forced a smile to her face as she opened the door. "Hello, Pastor Edwards. What are you doing in this neighborhood today? Come on in, sit down, make yourself at home. Can I get you a cup of coffee of tea?"

Pastor Edwards smiled and briskly shook her hand. "No, Mrs. Perkins, I'm really not thirsty. I was just out in the area, and I thought I'd stop by and see how you've been doing. It seems like forever since I've seen you at the church, and I'm worried about you." He sat down on the sofa, and Mrs. Perkins sat down in her rocking chair.

She laughed nervously before replying, "Why you didn't need to worry. I've just been having some trouble getting over that back surgery I had, and I still can't sit still for any length of time without my back really hurting me. My doctor told me it wasn't good for me to sit in one position for any length of time, and I can't drive, so I haven't been coming to church."

Looking concerned, he commented, "I am so sorry to hear you've been having trouble. We've missed you, you know. And, you've been in our prayers Your friends are constantly asking where you are. They'll be glad to hear that I visited with you. They'll want to come visit you too, what could you like me to tell them it's OK to visit?"

He leaned toward her expectantly, but she just didn't know what to say. She couldn't really afford to have any company because then she couldn't take her medicine and drink her medicinal alcohol. She'd have to think of something to tell him, and fast. She sighed before responding. "Oh, well thank you for your prayers. My doctor wants me to get lots of rest, so I'd appreciate it if you told everyone that I'm not quite up to receiving visitors quite yet. I'm grateful for the thought, though, and I'll be sure to let you know when I am able to have visitors," She didn't know quite what else to say, so she looked down at her hands She picked at a hangnail. The silence seemed to last forever, and the quiet was unnerving.

Finally Pastor Edwards cleared his throat. As he was getting up, he said, "Well, Molly, I can see that you're not feeling well. I'd better get going so you can get back to your rest."

She slowly got to her feet; she had to see him to the door. Halfway there she felt herself slipping, and everything was going black around her as she fell to the floor. She was barely aware of the pastor reaching towards her and of her own voice mumbling "Dizzy" before she lost consciousness.

The next day she woke up in her hospital room. A nurse had just entered her room and announced that it was time to check her blood pressure. Molly shook her head; she was really feeling quite groggy. She couldn't remember coming to the hospital, and she was becoming increasingly apprehensive. What was she doing here? Why was she here? How had she got here? Why couldn't she remember? She turned towards the nurse to ask her and was hit by a barrage of pain. She involuntarily cried out, and the nurse was instantly at her side. She found herself gasping for air, and in between gasps she was trying to tell the nurse she needed something for pain. The nurse told her she could have some Tylenol now that she was awake. Dear God, what was she going to do about the pain? She couldn't get her pills or her medicinal alcohol in here. How was she going to survive?

* * * * *

It had been an extremely long day for Molly. The Tylenol hadn't touched her back pain or her arthritic pain. The doctor had finally ordered Demerol injections, but the nurses acted like they'd rather die than give her a pain shot. They were all rude and demeaning. They all called her "Molly" or, worse yet, "Honey" or "Sweetie". She might just as well be a mannequin lying here. She'd push the "nurse" button on her siderail, and, if she was lucky, some secretarial, ward clerk type would respond within a few minutes. She always promised to "tell the nurse," but Molly always had to push the button several more times and wait over an hour before she got the pain medication she'd initially requested.

Once, at change of shift when the nurses were making rounds, she heard them talking outside her door. They didn't know she was listening, and she heard them refer to her as a "drug addict". So that was what they thought of her! How dare they refer to her that way! It had taken her a long time to get over her anger. And, if the pain hadn't been so bad, she would have checked out of this place. Imagine, nurses like that had no business taking care of people. Everyone knew drug addicts hung out on street corners and shot up with dirty needles. She hadn't been born yesterday. She knew about drug addicts. The very idea of calling her a drug addict was ridiculous!

Molly woke up in the middle of the night. There was something crawling on her, and it hadn't worked when she'd tried to fling it off in her sleep. That was what had awakened her. She reached for light and turned it on. She gasped, there were bugs crawling all over her. She had to get the nurse. What kind of hospital was this anyway? This time, when they finally answered her call button , she was screaming for help. And this time they were there in a hurry. Why couldn't she get rid of these bugs? And why couldn't she stop shaking? She was having trouble telling what was real and what wasn't.....it was like everything was happening through a fog. Even so, she could tell the nurses were worried. That meant something must really be wrong. What was going on with her? Why didn't they do something about it?

This bug-filled nightmare seemed to go on forever, but finally a nurse walked in and gave her a shot. This one put her to sleep. Molly didn't know how long she'd slept. All she knew was she was hungry. They'd said they'd get her lunch to her as soon as they could when she'd buzzed them. Then, before she knew it, there was a woman coming in the door to her room.. She had a tray in her hand, but she wasn't wearing a uniform. She must have noticed the questioning look Molly was giving her, because she stopped halfway to Molly's bed and introduced herself.

"Hello Mrs. Perkins. I'm Ms. Larson. I'm a certified chemical dependency nurse specialist, and I work here in the hospital as a psychiatric clinical nurse specialist. The nurses here on your unit phoned in a nursing consult to me and asked me to come see you. I stopped at the desk, to let them know I was here, and they asked me to bring your lunch tray with me. Where would you like me to set it?"

Molly was too stunned to answer for a minute. Psychiatric. That one word told her they must think she was crazy. After what had happened the last time she was awake, they might be right. Finally, she swallowed and said, "Over there on the bedside table will do."

Ms. Larson smiled as she set down the tray and said, "Mind if I sit down and we talk for a few minutes?"

She felt like a captive audience, so Molly agreed. They talked about the weather for a few minutes while Molly ate some of her lunch. Finally, Molly relaxed enough to get up her courage to ask, "Do you mind telling me again why you're here? I didn't quite catch it the first time."

"Well, Mrs. Perkins, last night you had what's know as delirium tremens. That's the medical term for when you see and feel things that aren't there and you get the shakes or have seizures. It happens when your body is used to having a steady supply of alcohol and all of a sudden that supply stops. Withdrawal from alcohol can kill you, so the nurses were concerned for your safety. They called your doctor and got an order for an intramuscular injection that prevented you from having seizures. They also sent me a consult asking me to come talk to you about the chance that you might be chemically dependent."

Molly's eyes got big. "What do you mean chemically dependent? If you think I'm a drug addict, you're dead wrong. I heard those nurses talking and calling me an addict. Last night before they gave me a shot, I thought I heard one tell another that 'she must be an alcoholic too'. The very idea! Don't they know I'm a lady? I don't live on the streets, and I don't shoot up or get falling down drunk. This is the most ridiculous thing I've ever heard!"

"Mrs. Perkins, I can understand your concern. Nobody is calling you a drug addict or a drunk. I'm here to get some idea of the medications you were taking and the amount of alcohol you were drinking before you came in the hospital. I realize that you only took legal, prescribed medications, and I'm guessing you started taking them with alcohol because it helped them do a better job of killing the pain."

Molly sighed. "Well, that's better. Of course I only took prescription medications. And you're right, the alcohol helped them work better. I have problems with arthritis, and since my back operation, I can't seem to control the pain from my back. Nothings' worked, so I just kept going to doctors and taking what they gave me."

The nurse leaned forward and asked. "What were you taking and how often?"

"Well," answered Molly. "I was taking two different pain pills and one tranquilizer with scotch and water about every four hours. Between doses, I was drinking a double scotch all by itself. It didn't exactly make the pain go away, but it dulled it, and I didn't care about it anymore."

The nurse responded, "Thank you for being so honest with me Mrs. Perkins. You were taking enough medication...and alcohol is a drug, too....that you had developed what we call 'dependence' and 'tolerance'. Dependence occurs when your body has to have a substance to keep from going into withdrawal from that substance. Tolerance occurs when you need more and more of the substance to get the same effect. What you experienced last night...the shakes and seeing and feeling things that weren't there...that's a form of alcohol withdrawal that I talked about earlier, delirium tremens."

Molly was listening closely. All she could manage in response was. "Oh." Then she remembered how frightened she'd been when her "withdrawal" reaction was happening. Before she thought, she found herself saying, "I was so scared. I'd never had anything like that happen before. I couldn't tell what was real and what wasn't. That doesn't mean I'm an addict or a drunk."

The nurse responded, "It must have been very frightening for you. I don't want you to get hung up on labels that have negative meanings for you. Let's forget the terms "addict" and "drunk" and "alcoholic". Instead, let's focus on the fact that you had some problems with prescribed medications in combination with alcohol. Sometimes, people take more of their medications or combine them in ways their doctor or doctors haven't ordered because what their doctor orders doesn't really give them pain relief. And, sometimes, they become dependent and develop tolerance as a result. Its like a side effect of their self-medication is chemical dependence, especially if they combine their medication with increasing use of alcohol."

Molly sat up and listened more closely. The nurse was describing what had happened to her.

"You mean what I have is a side effect of me taking all those medications at once with my scotch and water."

The nurse nodded "yes". Molly looked puzzled, then she asked, "Well, how do I get rid of this side effect?"

The nurse smiled before replying, "First we find out how much medication you need to give you relief from your pain. Then we give you smaller and smaller doses along with smaller and smaller doses on an "as needed" basis of medication that will keep you from having alcohol withdrawal. At the same time, we teach you different pain management techniques. Once you're over your withdrawal, we get you enrolled in an outpatient chemical dependence treatment program. I'll be seeing you everyday while you're in the hospital, and I'll work with you on learning how to manage your pain. When you're discharged, I'll go with you to the outpatient chemical dependence treatment program to introduce you to the staff there and to make sure your transition to outpatient treatment goes smoothly. If you want, you and I can continue to have weekly sessions with each other on an outpatient basis."

Molly was confused. This sounded like a lot of bother. She wasn't sure she really understood. On one hand, the nurse was telling her she was not an addict or drunk and that she only had side effects from self-medicating in combination with alcohol. On the other hand, it sounded like she was telling her she needed out patient treatment in a program for addicts and alcoholics. Yet, she liked this nurse. She seemed to know what she was talking about. She decided to level with her.

"I don't understand. First you tell me I'm not an addict or drunk, that I have side-effect problems with prescribed medications in combination with alcohol, and then, almost in the next breath, you tell me I need outpatient treatment in a program that treats alcoholics and addicts."

The nurse chuckled. "You're right Mrs. Perkins. Maybe what we need to talk about here is that having problems with alcohol and drugs is not a moral issue. Chemical dependence is a disease...not a choice, not a weakness, and not a sin. It's the same disease whether you've got problems with prescribed medications, scotch, beer, or heroin. It's an equal opportunity disease that strikes all sexes, all ages, and all socioeconomic classes. Not all alcoholics are homeless bums. Not all drug addicts use hypos to shoot up illegal drugs. Some people develop chemical dependency by taking increasingly large doses...or the same dose more often... of prescribed medications. The way you get there doesn't matter as much as what you're willing to do to get better."

The nurse took a deep breath before continuing, "Maybe it'd help you if you knew that I consider myself a recovering drug addict and alcoholic. Twenty years ago when I went through my basic nurses training everyone was dropping acid and smoking pot. It was a fact of life. Later, I learned to drink with my colleagues after work and on weekends to forget the stress we experience in our work. Finally, I started having blackouts...forgetting things that happened when I drank that I should have been able to remember... and I ended up having to be treated for chemical dependence on alcohol and Valium. I'm not proud of having had to face my own chemical dependence, but it does help me understand how hard it is to face it in the beginning."

The nurse stood up before continuing. "You look tired. I'll go so you can rest. I'll be back tomorrow at the same time and we can talk some more. You've got a lot to think about, and I want to give you time to think about it. I don't want us to get stuck on arguing about whether or not you're chemically dependent. What matters is you have a problem with your drug and alcohol use. The alcohol withdrawal you experienced last night could have killed you if you hadn't been in a hospital where you got immediate treatment for it. It's not important what we call what you have or how you got there. It is important to figure out what you're going to do about it....how you're going to get out of the problem and into the solution. If you need to talk, have the nurse call me. Otherwise, I'll be here for our appointment tomorrow."

Then the nurse smiled, turned, and walked out of Molly's room. Molly laid back on her pillow. She certainly did have a lot to think about.

Chapter XIV

ACCEPTANCE and SEXUALITY

Maggie was early. It was her turn to make the coffee before the meeting started. As she filled the pot with water, she remembered the coffee pot that had been at the outpatient treatment center where she'd been treated for her alcoholism. It had been as old and worn as this one. Maggie didn't like to think about that time in her life. It had been the first time she let herself trust a group. And it had been a mistake.

She remembered how everyone had shared their "life story" with the others in the group. Common themes of trust, confidentiality, honesty and unconditional love kept emerging. Even though others shared deeply personal things, she still couldn't bring herself to be honest with the group about herself. Honesty had cost her friends before, and she cared enough about this group not to risk their rejection.

Her counselor had spent hours trying to get her to be honest in her individual sessions. Finally, she'd broken down and told everything to her counselor. To her amazement, her counselor hadn't batted an eyelid. She remembered thinking maybe there was something to this unconditional love thing after all.

There was one group where everyone took turns "sitting in the hot seat". That meant the entire group focused on one member until they broke through the person's defenses and his or her raw emotions were exposed. Maggie had to admit that the therapist had been very good at getting the group to help the person in the hot seat to "put the pieces back together" before the session ended. Everybody who'd been there as long as Maggie had already had their turn. Now it was Maggie's turn and she was scared. She knew Pete had talked about his guilt over his many adulterous affairs. Tanya had talked about being the victim of incest. George had talked about the guilt he couldn't get rid of because he'd accidentally killed his wife and child in a car accident he'd caused by driving while intoxicated. Bert had talked about how hard it'd been to tell his wife he had Aids from shooting up with dirty needles. Sally had talked about shoplifting and being a prostitute so she could afford her habit. Nobody had talked about being gay.

Maggie was sitting in the hot-seat. She heard the rain striking the windows, the coffee pot groaning, and the clock ticking. The silence was overwhelming. She had to start. She might as well start with something they'd already talked about in this group.

She cleared her throat. "It started for me when I was about 10. My father would come home drunk and beat my mother. She stopped sleeping with him. Several months later he started coming in my room at night and 'playing with my privates' as he put it. He took pictures. Not just of me all naked and exposed but also of us together. He told me he'd show them to my mother if I told anyone. He told me it'd kill her to find out, and he told me he'd kill me if I told anyone. You couldn't see my face in some of the pictures they were close-ups of anatomical parts that could have belonged to anyone. But my face was clearly visible in some of them. So I believed him. I kept quiet. I got to where my mind would go somewhere else every time I heard him turn the doorknob."

Maggie took a sip of the coffee. Then she started talking again. "He made a big deal about me not dating anyone. I was so turned off by men by then he didn't need to worry. Once in a while I'd risk bringing girl friends home with me after school because he'd be away at work. Sometimes I got really brave and had them stay over night. I learned that he stayed away from me on those nights when I had company over."

They were all looking intently at her. She had to finish. "I started drinking when I got to college. Somehow it made it easier to live with all those memories. I found my self hanging out at women's bars."

She stopped. She heard one sharp intake of breath. She might as well get this over. "I finally had the nerve to go home with one of the lesbians I met in a bar one night. I had my first orgasm that night. Letty and I were a couple after that night for several years. My drinking got worse. She finally left me for another woman. To hear her tell it, it was all because of my drinking. She may have been right. I know I'd started fighting with her whenever I drank. A couple of times I hit her. I hated myself the most then because I reminded myself of my father. So in a way I was relieved when she left me. I started being a real loner at work, but I entered what I call my 'promiscuous stage. That's fancy talk for a lot of one night stands.

The group was clearly uncomfortable with what she was saying. Several members were not able to look her in the face. When she looked at them they looked down. Somehow she got the courage to continue.

"My drinking got worse. I started missing work. Finally I lost my job. I managed to get multiple DWIs. Then I got arrested at the bar one night for making a scene with one of the women at the bar. She thought I was trying to move in on her woman. I might have been. I'll never know because I have no memory of that night. They tell me she pulled a knife on me and that I was lucky the police broke it up when they did. In my sober moments I missed Letty and the special moments we'd shared. She'd been so thoughtful and romantic, and I'd thrown it all away with my drinking. I was very down myself. The guilt and despair were awful. One night I washed down a full bottle of Valium with a bottle of scotch. I woke up in intensive care. When I could be discharged they sent me here."

The quietness of the group was noticeable. Again, Maggie heard the rain, the groaning coffee pot, and the ticking clock. Where was the "unconditional love" they'd promised? Finally, Tanya broke the silence. She didn't look at Maggie. Instead she looked at the therapist. Then she said. "I want a new roommate. I can't share a room with a lesbo."

The others had been nicer. They'd said the right things. The things people usually said at the end of such groups to help "put the pieces back together" again. After that group, no one sought her out to talk to anymore. No one sat by her in group or in the dining room. Everyone was polite. Just barely. She'd been ready to leave the treatment center "against medical advice", but her counselor talked her into taking a pass to go to an AA meeting. She'd said it was a special meeting and that she had wanted to process Maggie's reaction to it before she discharged her.

Maggie's thoughts were disrupted by the sounds of laughter. Jonelle and Mary Ann were just coming in the door for the meeting. She hugged both of them "hello". Then there were others to greet. It was time for the meeting to start. Maggie had also volunteered to chair the meetings this month since she knew she'd be there to make coffee.

Maggie started the meeting the usual way by having everyone join her in saying the Serenity Prayer. Then they read “How It Works” from the first three pages of Chapter 5 in Alcoholic Anonymous "Big Book". Maggie asked if anyone had a topic they needed to talk about. When nobody volunteered a topic, she introduced the one she'd chosen.

"As I was making the coffee, I was remembering what led me to this meeting the first time. My counselor was worried about me. I talked about my drinking in a group, and I'd been honest for the first about being a lesbian. So, the others who were in treatment at the time had stopped having anything to do with me. My roommate requested a new roommate. She thought I might try to turn her into a lesbian. I was angry and hurt. I wanted to leave the treatment program before my counselor thought I should. I know why now. In my anger and hurt I was ripe for relapse. Before she let me sign myself out, she made me come to this meeting."

Maggie had noticed several empathetic nods as she talked. She smiled as she continued, "I guess the topic I'm trying to introduce is one that's pretty basic to this group. That's how to be gay and stay sober in a straight world that condemns our sexuality. I know its one we've talked about before. We have several newcomers to our group tonight, and I think it would help them to hear our experiences with this topic. Those who spoke on this topic the night I first showed up to this group helped me. They gave me the courage to go back to my counselor and begin the work of dealing with my own issues in spite of my peers' reaction to my sexuality. It would have been altogether too easy to use that as an excuse to start drinking and using again. She and some of you in this group helped me get beyond that first reaction into some hard won recovery. I've talked enough, who'd like to go first?"

Harold was the first to speak up, "I had a similar reaction when I was a patient in a hospital based treatment center. I was in a VA hospital with a bunch of macho Vietnam vets. You can imagine their delight in learning that they were sharing quarters with a queer. We didn't know much about AIDS in those days, and they were all convinced that they'd get AIDS just from breathing the same air. I was lucky I didn't get beat up. I was lucky. There was a nurse there that made a difference. Actually, he probably saved my life. Because, like you, without his intervention I would have relapsed. And the doctors had told me that with my history of pancreatitis, I'd die if I drank again."

"He had the courage to take all those vets on in a group. He told them that the only dues for AA membership was alcoholism. That the fellowship was extended to anyone who had a desire to stop drinking. He told them if they didn't believe that....if they didn't practice that philosophy in their attempts to get sober well then, they could kiss their chance at sobriety and the joys of recovery good-bye. At first they ignored him. Then he brought in guest speakers who wowed them with stories of their successful sobriety. These were upstanding, manly specimens of male sobriety. They shared their stories and won the respect and admiration of the group. Then after the panel presentation was over they one by one took turns talking again. This time around, they all talked about being both sober and gay. You could have heard a pin drop. But you know it was worth it. It worked. Especially when one of the men, a retired Marine, told how he'd saved his platoon from certain death. One of the straight guys even ended up sharing how a gay comrade had lost his life to save his in one battle. After that, they started accepting me as a person first, an alcoholic second, and lastly as a gay person. If it hadn't been for that nurse, none of them would have ever bothered to give me the time of day again."

Sandra spoke up next. "I was never honest about my sexuality while I was in treatment. I waited until I'd been in recovery several years. Then I let my doctor videotape an interview with me for a videotape he was making about sexuality and recovery. He wanted to show that sexual issues were a part of normal recovery. He initially wanted me to make the point that I experimented with gay sex as part of my recovery before I returned to the fold and proclaimed my return to heterosexuality. It was a good illustration of how biased the psychiatric profession can be about homosexuality even though they've taken it out of their precious revised DSM IV. I refused to alter the truth to support his theories. We went round and round, but finally he had to admit that homosexuality was a healthy option for women in sobriety. He actually ended up learning from me and my case history. So, there I am in the middle of his videotape proclaiming sobriety and homosexuality can be normal, healthy options for some people. I did talk about promiscuity as one of the stages I had to come through in my own personal sexual growth process. I made it clear that was more related to my history of being an incest victim that to my homosexuality. All in all, it felt very good to be instrumental in helping the psychiatric profession learn about homosexuality and sobriety as healthy alternatives."

Evidently that struck a nerve for one of the newcomers. "Hi, I'm Joe, and I'm an alcoholic. I'm glad you brought that up, Sandra. My doctor keeps trying to convince me that my homosexuality is just a phase I'm going through. I get the feeling he won't pronounce me 'cured' unless I 'see the light' and 'return' to a heterosexual lifestyle . I can't get him to understand that it's impossible for me to return to heterosexuality. He can't seem to understand that I've always been homosexual. He doesn't understand that it's a matter of genetics and biology. I was born this way. My homosexuality is as normal for me as my brown eyes. Sure, I could get colored lenses and change the color of my eyes. Blue eyes would probably be more valued by the most of society. I like my brown eyes. I also like my sexuality. Why should I try to change either trait just to please part of society? God, am I glad I found this Lamboda group. Now I know I'm not crazy. It's society and psychiatry that have been a problem accepting me for who and what I am. Thank you for helping me see that!"

There was a prolonged moment of silence. A couple of people got up and helped themselves to more coffee. Then Thelma spoke up.

"My experience has been a little different. Chris was an alcoholic too. She'd even been married to a gay man. She didn't trust men, so she turned to the comfort of the company of women. She convinced herself that she was a lesbian. She had experimented with several women while she was still drinking. Then, several years into her recovery she met me. We were together for several years when she started feeling attracted to men. She started seeing a therapist. She told me she was leaving me because she wanted me to find someone who could really love me. All this time, she'd been telling me she loved me. You can imagine how that hurt. She kept saying she loved me, but she wasn't in love with me. I didn't understand what she meant until I broke up this last time with the woman I met after Chris left me. I found myself saying the same thing to her. I've been seeing a therapist. Now I'm able to see that it's not fair to either partner to stay in a relationship when one stops being in love with the other. And she'd helped me realize that I still love this woman as a friend. But, back to my point, Chris found out in her therapy that she really was heterosexual. That can happen once in a while, but it's usually the exception. Most of us are born this way. Chris was different. For her, women were a stage she went through before she could face her heterosexuality and stay sober. She'd always been drinking before when she related to a male sexually. Her therapist helped her see that for her homosexuality had been a way to protect her from facing trust issues related to her being the victim of incest at the hand of her grandfather when she was a child. A breakthrough came for Chris when she started having flashbacks about those time, while a man was making love to her. She was sober at the time, so she could feel it and remember it. then she processed it with her therapist. Chris and I are friends now. I realize she did what she had to do. I'm talking about this so the newcomers will know that even though there's pressure sometimes from the psychiatric profession to favor heterosexuality over homosexuality there's sometimes pressure from the gay community to favor homosexuality over heterosexuality. The Big Book tells us this is a program of honesty, so I felt it was important to say that for each of us our sexuality is a very personal and unique aspect of our lives... one that each one of us has to explore and come to accept as it is regardless of how our counselors, therapists or friends advise us. The program tells us there are some things we can't change and the Serenity Prayer asks for courage to accept those things. Our sexuality, be it heterosexuality or homosexuality, happens to be one of those things."

The room was quiet. After several minutes of silence, Maggie found herself saying. "Thelma, it took courage to say that in a room full of gay people. Thank you for helping us apply our program's concept of acceptance where it is sometimes the most difficult. Is there anyone who has a burning desire to share something?"

After several moments, nobody had spoken up. So Maggie closed the meeting by saying. "OK, lets close the meeting in the regular way . Will those of you who wish to do so, join hands and join me in the Lord's Prayer."

Maggie stayed after the meeting to help clean up and to take care of the coffee pot. To her surprise, she realized that she was grateful for what had happened to her while she was in treatment. Because of that, she'd been able to talk about it. So, it had been a good meeting. She wouldn't have admitted it at the time, but her Higher Power had known exactly what She was doing.

Chapter XV

IT'S POSITIVE

It was raining. Again. It had been raining for a week. If this kept up, Chuck was afraid he'd forget what the sun looked like. I'm tired of being cooped up inside. It's been over a week now, and being shut in with all these loonies is getting to me. Not that I feel like going outside. I feel like I have the flu or something. Come to think of it, I've felt that way for quite a while now. I felt like that even before I came into the hospital. At first, I thought it was a reaction to coming off the heroin. That had been an ordeal, but it was over now and he still felt bad.

They had an outing planned this afternoon to a Narcotic's Anonymous (NA) meeting that was close by in the neighborhood. At least I'll finally get out of this place for a while. I wonder how many people I'll see there that I know from the streets. Really, when you think about it, its ironic that I ended up doing this whole drug treatment gig anyway. I certainly didn't plan on drying out, but when my probation officer gave me a choice between doing more time or drying out, getting treatment sounded like a good idea.

His thoughts were interrupted by a knock on his door. Pete, the day nurse, stuck his head through Chuck's door and said "Chuck, your doctor wants to see you before you go to group. Group starts in about 20 minutes, so you need to get a move on man."

Good thing he'd already dressed. Guess he'd have to put off going outside for that smoke. "Sure thing, Pete. I'm on my way."

With that he got up off his bed and walked out of the room. "Wait up, Pete. Do you know what he wants to talk to me about? My appointment's not until this afternoon after we get back from the NA meeting."

Pete looked thoughtful before answering, "He didn't say." Both he and Pete stopped at the coffee pot in the day room to get a cup of coffee. Whatever it was his doctor wanted to talk to him about, it would wait at least long enough for him to score some caffeine.

As soon as Chuck knocked on the door, he heard Dr. Allen's deep voice say, "Yes. Come in." Chuck looked around his doctor's office as he walked through the door. Dr. Allen had a fish tank that filled up an entire wall. On the other wall he had all these ethnic looking wall hangings. Then there were the weird looking sculptures placed strategically around the room along with an occasional fake plant here and there. It was like this guy couldn't decide to be genuine and natural or phony and showy. Chuck had to laugh at himself. Here he was in a shrink's office analyzing his shrink.

Dr. Allen must have heard Chuck laugh under his breath because he immediately asked. "What's got you laughing this morning Chuck?"

Chuck knew he couldn't be entirely honest. So he replied, "Oh something one of the fellows said earlier to me at breakfast. One of those delayed-action joke things." Chuck sat down in the stuffed chair next to Dr. Allen's desk. That put him facing Dr. Allen at about a forty-five degree angle. Chuck remembered learning in some psychology class that facing someone at a forty-five degree angle enhanced communication. That was because it allowed "comfortable eye contact"...that facing someone head on and having to always look them straight in the face was often uncomfortable and could, in fact, shut down communication. Amazing the things you remembered sometimes.

It had been years since Chuck finished college. There'd been no jobs available for someone with a bachelor's degree in psychology, so he' wandered from odd job to odd job and had finally fallen in with the drug using crowd, it just seemed like the easiest thing to do. He'd been young and impressionable then, and he'd wanted to "go where the action was". He had to admit that it had all been pretty exciting at first.

He'd got into the music business playing his sax in one band after another in the night clubs all over town, and he'd learned first hand that musicians and dope were almost synonymous. It had been years later when it all caught up with him and he'd started having to steal and pimp to support his habit. By then the excitement had worn off and it had all become just a matter of survival on the streets.

Dr. Allen cleared his throat. That meant he was about to say something of some import. Chuck looked closely at him and said, "I'm all ears Doc. What's on your mind?"

Dr. Allen cleared his throat again. "Well, Chuck. I need to talk to you about your lab results. We did the usual admission lab work on you that we do with all patients. One of those lab tests with our addicts is a routine test for HIV antibodies. Yours came back positive for HIV antibodies.

Chuck didn't like the sound of this. Not at all. He set his cup of coffee down on the Doc's desk before he replied, "What are you tryin' to say Doc? You tryin' to tell me I have Aids or what?"

Chuck was leaning forward in his chair, as he looked down he realized he'd clenched his hands into tight fists. He must be pretty anxious. Damn right! It wasn't everyday some shrink told you that you had Aids. That was like getting a death sentence, and he just wasn't ready to hear that. Dr. Allen still hadn't answered him. His silence said it all.

Chuck shook his head emphatically, "no". Then he started talking to Dr. Allen again. "No way Doc. You've got it all wrong. They must have made some mistake with the lab work. Got mine mixed up with someone else's. Happens all the time. Besides, I'm no faggot. There's no way I could have Aids.

Dr. Allen Looked real serious. He looked at Chuck as he spoke, "There's been no mistake, Chuck. We're real careful about these things. We have to be. We've even done the confirmation test. I wouldn't be telling you this if we weren't sure. Besides, your history fits the picture."

Chuck impatiently interrupted, "What do you mean, 'fits the picture'. I already told you, I'm no faggot!"

Dr. Allen answered, " That's not what I mean Chuck. You don't have to be a homosexual to get Aids. You can get Aids from sharing dirty needles or from heterosexual or homosexual sex when you don't use a condom. You yourself told me there's been times you used in 'shooting galleries' where needle sharing was a common practice. When Pete did the patient teaching group on cleaning rigs, you told the group that all that Clorox water rigmarole was for the birds and a waste of time, that no one bothered to take the time or trouble to do that when they were wasted. So, we know you've probably been exposed."

Chuck was getting pissed off, "What do you mean exposed? I don't shoot up with faggots. I don't hang around with queers." Chuck felt like picking up his coffee cup and flinging it all over the doctor. Who did he think he was sitting there preaching about using dirty needles and engaging in what he and those like him referred to as "unprotected sex"?

Dr. Allen stayed calm as he replied, "Chuck, I know this is hard to take. This is pretty frightening stuff. No one is accusing you of being gay or of hanging around with gay men. Aids is not a punishment for being gay, for being a prostitute, or for using dirty needles. It's your body's response to a virus. Just like a lot of colds and flu are. In this case its much more serious because it wipes out your body's immune system and you can get sick very easily. Unfortunately, people usually die from illnesses they catch because they have no way to fight them off."

Chuck was quiet. This was a lot to digest. He knew that his denial and anger were normal responses to a crisis like this. He might feel a little better if he focused on getting information about his condition so he could start understanding it. If he understood it, maybe he'd feel a little less hopeless and helpless and a little more in control. Sometimes he was sorry he'd taken all that psychology. He was bitterly aware that he'd just flipped into using intellectualization as yet another defense mechanism.

Chuck had spent the rest of his day in his room. He'd not gone to any of the groups or therapies. He hadn't eaten. He'd spent the time thinking. And reading all the material about AIDs that Dr. Allen had given him. This was one time he wished he followed his counselor's advice and got a sponsor. He really needed someone from the streets to talk to now, someone who'd understand. But then how many people really did understand AIDs? Who could he talk to without being labeled as just another faggot or junkie? He really felt like his life was unmanageable. How ironic. He wondered if the AA founders knew just how unmanageable things could get when they first formulated AA's first step. "We admitted we were powerless over alcohol---that our lives had become unmanageable."[1]

His counselor had told him when he'd worked on his first step that a person could substitute any word for alcohol in that first step. He'd said you could even substitute the phrase "life itself" for "alcohol", and you'd still be right on target with the first step. He had to admit he was powerless over being positive for HIV antibodies and that his life was, as a result, extremely unmanageable. He didn't know what to expect. He had seen movies of people becoming increasingly ill and miserable and gradually wasting away and dying.

Dr. Allen had told him things were a little different now that they had medication that helped people who had the antibodies lead almost normal lives. He said they were able to stay alive much longer and to experience a much better quality of life than when AIDs had first arrived on the scene and they didn't know how to treat it.

Chuck had read all the material over and over. He knew all about the treatment and the signs and symptoms of some of the illnesses he'd need to watch out for. But where did he go from here? He couldn't stay in this room forever. He'd done about all he could by himself without going crazy. He'd promised Mike, his primary nurse, that if he ever had a crisis while he was in the hospital that he'd have the nurse on duty call him. This qualified as a

---

[1] Alcoholics Anonymous: Third Edition, New York: Alcoholics Anonymous, 1976: p. 59.

crisis, so maybe he should have her call him even if it was already past midnight.

Mike had got there within 15 minutes of Chuck having the nurse call. They'd taken a thermos of coffee into Mike's office and talked for several hours. Mike had even let him smoke in the office rather than making him go outside. They'd spent most of the time figuring out how Chuck could apply AA's first three steps to his situation. It had taken Chuck a long time to take the second step because right now he was pretty mad at his Higher Power. The second step, "Came to believe that a Power greater than ourselves could restore us to sanity",[2] seemed like a bitter pill to swallow right now. How could he trust a God that had let him catch the precursor to AIDs?

At first, Chuck had felt like there was this cosmic overlord who was getting into playing nasty games with him solely for the sake of amusing himself. How else could any infinite being take away your sanity by giving you an almost certain death sentence and then be trusted to give you your sanity back? That was before Mike had told him his Father had been really bitter about being diagnosed with both prostate and colon cancer for over a year. He hadn't started to enjoy the years of life he had left until Mike had got him involved in Alanon and a sponsor had taught him how to use the second and third step to help himself cope with his cancer. Mike had pointed out that the two steps hadn't cured the cancer or saved his life in the long haul. They had given him the gift of a serene and spiritually comfortable life until he died.

Chuck had finally realized that no one really knew how long they'd live or what they'd experience before they died and that improving his quality of life was probably an important thing for him to focus on...as it would be for anyone. When that had happened, Mike then said, "You may not realize it now Chuck, but you've just taken the second step. You've stopped blaming your higher power for giving you antibodies. You've started thinking about how you can let him help you live with it to the best of your ability."

They'd talked about that for a long time. Chuck had finally been willing to let go of all the anxiety and fear he'd been feeling all day by turning it over to his Higher Power. Mike helped him realize that none of us can ever really control other people, places of things....and that one of the best ways to do that is to take the third step. Mike had read the third step to him

[2] Ibid.

from the Big Book: "Make a decision to turn our will and our lives over to the care of God as *we understood Him.*"[3]

Finally, after they'd finished off the pot of coffee, Mike had yawned, and said. "Let's call it a night, pal. You've done a lot of hard work tonight. You've come a long way in working your NA program. You'd only taken the first step before tonight, and that was about your addiction. Now, you've taken the first two steps within the context of your entire life. That means you've used them to deal with both your addiction and your illness. You've accomplished a lot, and you still have a lot to think about. Sleep on it, and we'll work on it some more tomorrow."

To his surprise, Chuck did feel sleepy. Earlier today he would have sworn he'd never be able to relax enough to sleep again. Maybe there was something to this serenity thing. He stood up and hugged Mike, "Thanks man for coming out at this hour and helping me deal with this. You'll never know what it means to me."

Chuck was in bed within fifteen minutes. His mind was still reeling. The last thing he remembered thinking as he drifted off to sleep was "I can't handle this alone God. It's all yours...you can have it."

Several days later, Chuck was ready to tell the other patients about his condition. He and Mike had done a lot of work. Mike had convinced him that he was ready to "go public". He was anxious about it, but he had to start someplace. Mike had started the community meeting by asking if anyone had anything they needed to talk about. No one else had volunteered, so Chuck made himself speak up.

"This is probably the hardest thing I've ever done, but I have something I need to talk about. Two days ago I found out I have AIDs antibodies. I just about went stark raving mad. Mike came to my rescue. He helped me use the first three steps to get beyond my shock and denial. I know now that the promises that are in the Big Book are really true. One of them talks about God doing for us what we can't do for ourselves.[4] I wouldn't be here now if that hadn't been true for me with this AIDs thing."

Chuck stopped and looked around the room. Everyone looked shocked. No one said anything. What if they thought he was gay? What if they all shunned him now because they were afraid of catching AIDs? What if they went out and told everyone? He had to calm himself down, so he repeated the serenity prayer to himself in his mind.

---

[3] Ibid.

[4] Alcoholics Anonymous: Third Edition, New York: Alcoholics Anonymous, 1976.

Cheryl was the first to speak up. . "This is hard to say. I don't mean anything personal. I like Chuck and all, but we have to all use the same drinking fountain you know. And some of the guys are concerned about playing basket ball and volley ball with him. They're afraid that he might get scratched and bleed on the ball. We're worried about catching AIDs from him."

The entire time Cheryl was talking, she avoided looking Chuck in the eyes; it was as if she was ashamed of what she was saying.

Then Jim spoke up. "Cheryl's right. We're all worried. We have to live with him, and we don't want to catch it."

Mike looked around the room. He saw lots of worried faces. He leaned forward in his chair before he began.

"I can understand your concern. Its important for me to do some patient teaching here. Based on what we know about AIDs, you can only catch it from prolonged exposure to body fluids. That means it's highly unlikely that you'd catch it from using the same drinking fountain or from handling a basketball that a drop of Chuck's blood might contaminate."

The room was quiet while Mike's words sank in. Cheryl was the one to break the silence.

"That's easy for you to say, but what do we really know about AIDs. How can we know its OK to live in the same environment with him? How can we know its safe to use the same drinking fountain, to touch him, or to use the same telephone?"

Chuck felt like dropping through the floor. He couldn't remember having felt so awkward and uncomfortable in his life before. He'd been afraid of this moment, and now it was every bit as bad as he'd anticipated. He thought these people had accepted him. They had accepted both him and his addiction, but they obviously couldn't accept him now that they knew he would probably develop AIDs. He had to get out of this situation.

He cleared his throat. "Mike, let me say something here. Its clear that I'm not wanted as part of this community anymore. I can arrange to be discharged today. I can find some NA meetings to go to in the community. They'll accept me as part of them as long as I'm not honest about my AIDs condition."

Mike shook his head before responding, "That won't be necessary Chuck. Give us 24 hours to think about it. This will need to be a group conscience call, and you shouldn't leave until the community as a group has decided its in the best interest of the community."

Chuck looked doubtful. So did Cheryl and several of the other patients. Mike spoke up again.

"Let me explain what I'm talking about. I'm going to read a passage from the 'Big Book'. I suggest that after I read it everyone take it to heart and meditate about what it says. We'll meet again tomorrow morning at this time in community meeting. Then we'll make a group decision about whether or not you should leave this community."

Several patients leaned forward to pay close attention to what Mike was going to say. Some turned to the page he'd identified in the "Big Books" (AA's Alcoholics Anonymous) that they carried with them.

Mike continued, "It says right here on page 86: 'When we retire at night we constructively review our day. Were we resentful, selfish, dishonest or afraid? Do we owe an apology? Were we kind and loving toward all? What could we have done better? Were we thinking of ourselves most of the time? Or were we thinking of what we could do for others...we must be careful not to drift into worry, remorse or morbid reflection, for that would diminish our usefulness to others. After making our review we ask God's forgiveness and inquire what corrective measures should be taken."

* * * * *

Mike started the community meeting the same way he had the day before. This time waiting to see if anyone had anything they needed to talk about was even harder for Chuck. He was going on his third silent repetition of the serenity prayer in his mind when Mack, another patient, got up and walked over to his chair. Now what, thought Chuck. Mack's voice was gruff as he said.

"Stand up, man."

Slowly Chuck stood up. Mack hugged him. Chuck couldn't see them, but there were two tears slowly traveling down Mack's cheeks. Chuck was aware that a tear had slipped out of his own eye. Then, all the patients stood up and walked over to Chuck. One by one they each hugged him. He'd never been hugged so much in all his life. Nor had hugs ever meant so much. And several were crying as they hugged him. Before all the hugs were done, Chuck was crying uncontrollably. And with the tears come a tremendous sense of relief and gratitude. God was handling for him what he couldn't himself.

UNIT FIVE

PROFESSIONAL AS CLIENT

Chapter XVI

SHERRY JAMES, STUDENT NURSE

Mark had just pulled into the parking lot when he noticed another student pulling into the lot. He probably wouldn't have noticed if he hadn't recognized the car. It was Sherry --- she was supposed to meet him at the Jigger last night for some "almost the end of the semester" celebrating. He had waited almost an hour and a half for her and she hadn't shown up. They'd made the date the weekend before when they'd been polishing off some six-packs and watching the Longhorns and Aggies battle it out on the football field.

"Hey Sherry," he hollered as he was climbing out of his car, "where were you last night? I was at the Jigger until almost eleven and you still hadn't shown up. You know it's not good for my ego to be stood up like that!" His joking tone didn't manage to hide his underlying irritation, and he saw Sherry do a double take as she turned to look at him.

"What on earth are you talking about Mark Jones? I had to study for this OB final we're going to be taking in a few minutes. I wouldn't have made a date for the night before a final. If I had been crazy enough to do such a thing, I wouldn't have reneged on it---you know I'm a party animal and I wouldn' stand a friend up. That's not my style either."

Mark didn't know what to make of it. Sherry seemed serious. She obviously didn't remember having made the date. Even talking about it hadn't jogged her memory. She obviously didn't have a clue. Strange. She was usually pretty sharp. She usually remembered things better than most of them.

Their clinical group had more or less fallen into the habit of asking her about medication side effects and dosages rather than looking them up themselves. She always remembered details like that. That's why it was so strange that she'd forget something like this.

They walked into the school together, and within a few minutes were seated in a classroom waiting for the professor to hand out the exams. As she was waiting Sherry kept trying to remember the date with Mark that he claimed she'd made with him. On the way in he'd told her they'd decided to get together last night during the football game. All she remembered about the game was getting so drunk the room would start spinning every time she closed her eyes. Then, the next thing she knew, Mark was standing at the foot of his bed calling her sleepyhead. He'd told her everyone else had left hours ago and had offered to let her stay overnight. She'd got up and driven home.

Sherry told herself she had to stop thinking about it or she'd blow this exam. Several times in the past few months she'd noticed similar mysterious memory problems. She even joked about them as her "memory glitches" when Tina, her roommate, teased her about them. They'd got so bad that people besides Tina were beginning to notice them too. A couple of times Tina had even suggested she go in and get a neuro workup done on herself. Maybe she would. But she kept worrying that somehow they were connected with her drinking. Tina had also suggested that possibility.

She remembered her psychiatric nursing instructor's lecture on alcoholism and how sometimes alcoholics would experience something called "blackouts." Sometimes when alcoholics were drinking they couldn't remember the details of entire blocks of time that had elapsed while they were drinking. During these so called blackouts the person appeared normal. Nobody could even tell anything was wrong. They were able to carry on entire conversations, drive, dance, etc. They just couldn't remember any of it afterwards. Enough. She could worry later. Right now she needed to concentrate on taking this exam.

Later that evening she and Tina went to the Jigger to celebrate surviving the OB final. Mark and Gary were there and the four of them made a night of it. Mark had teased her unmercifully about her standing him up the night before. She took it for a long time, but then it started getting to her because it made her think about the topic of blackouts again. Her father had been an alcoholic, and she couldn't stand the thought of being one too. She knew she ran a higher risk of being an alcoholic because her father was. That didn't make it any easier to contemplate the possibility of being one herself.

Evidently Mark could tell he was getting to her with the teasing because he finally stopped. They drank a lot, and they danced a lot. Before she knew it Tina was telling her it was time for them to go home. Tina wanted her to let her drive, but Sherry wasn't about to do that. That would mean admitting she was drunk. That was just too close to admitting she might have an alcohol problem.

On the way home, she dropped a cigarette while she was driving. She started reaching for it on the floor. Consequently, she had trouble getting the car to stay in their lane. Once she almost met a car head on before Tina grabbed the wheel and got them back over. Tina had been real quiet because she was scared. Now she decided she couldn't afford to be quiet any longer. She'd rather Sherry get mad at her than for the both of them to get messed up in some accident.

"Sherry, pull over. Let me drive. Its no big deal. You want to get home don't you."

Sherry giggled. "No way, Jose. I'm having fun. Look at this as an adventure. Just then they both heard the siren. Looking back, Tina and Sherry saw the revolving red and blue lights coming up behind them.

"Shit, I've done it now. Now I have to pull over. I've driven this way hundreds of times before and nothing has happened. Just my rotten luck!"

Sherry knew she needed to hold herself together in front of the cop. This was going to be hard to pull off. Sherry ended up spending the night in the local "drunk tank". It had been an experience she'd never forget. It had been all she could do to stagger into her room and collapse on her bed when she finally made it home. She slept for hours, oblivious that she was missing the final from the pain elective she'd taken this semester.

Tina was worried. She knew about Sherry's father and about Sherry's problems with blackouts. Now she was getting DWIs and missing school. At this rate, she wouldn't make it through nursing school. She'd been worried for quite some time. Something had to be done, she just wasn't sure what.

Tina sat and nursed her cup of coffee. There had to be something she could do. Being nice, making excuses for her roommate's increasingly inappropriate behavior, trying to talk her roommate into stopping drinking...none of it had helped. She remembered the lecture they had last semester on alcoholism. Her teacher had talked about things family members did to try to cover up for the problem that actually made the problem worse. She'd called it "enabling", and she'd given calling your alcoholic spouse's employer with excuses for their absences from work as an example. Maybe that's what she'd been doing with Sherry.

She had another sip of coffee. Maybe I'm on to something here, she thought. There was something families and employers did that sometimes helped, and her teacher had talked about how that procedure had also been adopted for use with impaired nurses in Texas. She'd even said it had also been used once with a student at their university.

She and Mark had talked just yesterday after the OB final about Sherry's problem with forgetting things. He'd seemed as worried about Sherry as Tina was after she explained it had happened several times and that her standing him up hadn't been just an isolated incident. He was good friends with her and Sherry. He could be trusted to keep all this confidential. She'd call him; maybe he'd have some ideas about what they could do to help Sherry. Maybe he'd be able to remember the name of the procedure that was eluding Tina.

Later that morning she dropped over to Mark's apartment. They'd decided to get together to talk about how they could help Sherry. Tina thought it was better to go over to Mark's than to run the risk of Sherry waking up and figuring out what she and Mark were doing. She'd left a note for Sherry saying she had decided to go over to Mark's to study for tomorrow's final.

Mark met her at the door. "Come on in; I've got a pot of coffee made. I also pulled out my notes from last semester. Maybe there's something in there that can help us figure out what to do." She walked in and sat down at Mark's kitchen table while he poured their coffee. "Great, that should really help. I've been racking my brain to try to remember some details about what Dr. Farwell said about that procedure that families and employers sometimes did with alcoholics to get them into treatment."

Mark made a face as he sat down. "Do you really think Sherry's an alcoholic Tina? She's just had this one DWI and some transient memory problems. I think its just some temporary stress thing."

Tina looked perplexed. "I'd like to think that Mark, but this has gone on for some time now. I've tried convincing myself it wasn't a major problem, but it won't go away. It just keeps getting worse. You haven't had to ride with her driving while intoxicated as often as I have. When she gets like that she won't let anyone else drive for love or money. She says its her way of proving she's OK and not just another alcoholic like her father."

"So, she's got drunk a few times and driven around. Happens all the time. Most of the people I know who drink have done that, and most of them have also had trouble remembering how they got home from time to time."

Tina could see she was getting nowhere trying to convince Mark that Sherry was an alcoholic. Something about that label brought out a lot of defensiveness in people. Earlier when she'd talked to him, he'd agreed with her that Sherry had a problem, but that was before she called it alcoholism.

Tina drank some more of her coffee before speaking again. "Mark, I don't think it matters so much what we call Sherry's problem. What is important is that we help her do something about it before it gets worse. Lets focus on figuring out what we can do to help."

Mark smiled, "You're right, Tina. Let's look through these notes for that procedure you're talking about."

They found it in Mark's notes right away. Dr. Farwell had called the procedure an intervention. She had said that it utilized a group of people to confront someone in a caring manner who had an addiction problem to break through that person's denial system and motivate him or her to seek treatment. Mark even had a reprint in his notes of an article Dr. Farwell and a former student had written. The article was about an intervention their university had done that helped that student get treatment for her alcoholism.[1]

Mark quickly scanned the article and handed each page to Tina as he finished it so she could do the same thing. After they finished, he poured them both another cup of coffee.

"Tina, I hate to admit it, but maybe you're right. Maybe Sherry's drinking has got to the point that we should consider doing something. We could just try talking to her ourselves about all this."

"We could try that, but I don't think it would work. When I try to get her to talk about it, she either gets mad and leaves the room or she gets quiet and refuses to talk to me for several hours. I'm at my wits end...I don't know where to go from here."

Mark thought for a minute before saying, "You know, I think we should call Dr. Farwell. She said that if any of us ever needed to talk about something like this, she would act as a resource and that everything would be kept confidential".

After they called Dr. Farwell, they went into talk to her. Dr. Farwell had helped them decide that Sherry really did need some help, and she helped them plan an intervention for Sherry. First, she asked them to identify any other close friends of Sherry's that might be willing to help and who had first hand knowledge of some of the problems that Sherry had been having. They had decided not to involve any instructors because Tina and Mark were fairly certain that none of the instructors had noticed any problems yet ... and by asking they would have broken the confidentiality that was key to this intervention approach working.

They were able to get the close friends together that very afternoon. Dr. Farwell asked them to try to remember any problems they'd observed Sherry having that might be related to having a problem with alcohol. She

---

[1] Sisney, K.F., Taylor, P. Conquering the Challenge of Student Chemical Dependence. Imprint 1991:38 (4), pp. 73-75.

also stressed the importance of everything that was said being kept in the strictest of confidence.

Sara was the first to speak up. "I was with Sherry at the frat party the night she fell down the stairs and broke her glasses. She'd been drunk at the time, but she just laughed it off and insisted on driving us both home anyway. I was afraid we weren't going to make it home in one piece that night."

Then Tina had shared with the group what had happened the night Sherry got picked up for the DWI. She stressed how scary and dangerous it had been.

Tom spoke up next. "I was in clinical with Sherry for the semester previous to this one. I smelled alcohol on her breath during start of shift report on two different occasions. She was also late to clinical several times...usually after we'd both been out drinking the night before."

Mark had been keeping quiet, but he decided to talk next. "Sherry and I have been friends for a long time now. Mostly drinking and dancing. Sherry loves to party. But lately its been catching up with her. She practically passed out over at my place the other night when we were drinking beer and watching football. But not before she made a date with me to meet me for drinks at the Jigger the night before the OB final. Then she stood me up. Never showed up. When I asked her about it the next day, she didn't remember even having made the date. Tina and I think she may be having blackouts."

Tina nodded her head in confirmation of what Mark had said. As they talked, her friends realized that they'd all made a mistake when they had assumed Sherry's drinking behaviors were just all part of her being just another "party animal". Now that they were together sharing their concerns and observations, a different picture was emerging. It was somewhat like putting a jigsaw puzzle together.

Looking at the overview this way, they agreed that Sherry did have a problem with alcohol ... that it was endangering not only her success as a student but her very life. That was when they realized the importance of what they were doing. Once they were convinced, Dr. Farwell asked their permission to bring in the associate dean so she could take part in the intervention and represent the Administration of the School. Someone from administration needed to be there so Sherry would understand that if she sought treatment she could remain in school and that the school would keep the intervention and her treatment confidential.

Dr. Farwell had also asked their permission to involve a psychologist from the university's student services department so she could be there to explain that the school had arranged a treatment package for Sherry that would let her get treatment over Christmas break as part of her student benefits. Dr. Farwell had said that having the treatment arranged to start immediately following the intervention was important because it didn't allow the person's defenses to build back up. It also got them directly into treatment when they were highly motivated and could really benefit from the treatment.

After the psychologist and associate dean arrived, Dr. Farwell had each of them write down what she called a "script". She had each of the students write out what they had personally observed and about their concerns. Then she had the associate dean write down what she was going to say about the consequences of Sherry's decision to seek treatment or not and how the school was going to respond to that decision. She had the psychologist write out what she was going to say about the two treatment options that had been arranged for Sherry.

Next, Dr. Farwell had them practice being an intervention team by using their scripts and role playing the confrontation while she played the part of Sherry. When they were done, Dr. Farwell smiled and said, "I think we're ready. Tomorrow is the last day of final's week, so we know Sherry will be here. She'll find a note in her mailbox summoning her to the dean's office. From there Dr. Terrill will take her to the administrative conference room. Are there any questions?"

Tina spoke up. "I know I said I'd take her to the hospital if she decides to seek treatment, but what if she refuses treatment?"

Dr. Farwell shook her head. "That's a good question Tina. It will be very important for at least one of you to stay with her after the intervention regardless of the outcome. She can't be left alone; that's because people sometimes become suicidal after an intervention. Such people often expect perfection from themselves and they are devastated by the idea that they might be an addict or an alcoholic."

* * * * *

Tina felt like she could cut the tension in the conference room with a knife. Everyone looked uncomfortable. The wait for Dr. Terrill to escort Sherry into the conference room was interminable. Just when she'd given up on the door ever opening again, Dr. Terrill opened the door and escorted Sherry into the room. She turned and spoke to Sherry.

"Sherry, I think you know everyone here with perhaps the exception of Dr. Brown from Student Services. Dr. Farwell is here to help us do an intervention on your behalf. She's going to be taking over from here"

Dr. Farwell smiled at Sherry before beginning. "Sherry, we're here today at the request of your friends. They care about you, and they asked me to facilitate an intervention for you. Why don't you have a seat over here and try to relax as much as you can. Everyone that's here is here because they care about you and they want to see things get better for you. Our purpose for doing this is to convince you that you have a problem and to help you get help for that problem."

Dr. Farwell paused before continuing. "Should you decide not to seek help for your problem, then a record of this proceeding will be given to the Dean of the School of Nursing who will decide whether or not to pursue further administrative action. Except for that exception, everything said in this room will be kept confidential. There's only one other thing I need to ask you before we start, and that is for you to remain quiet and listen while everyone else takes their turn talking. After everyone else has talked, it will be your turn to say what you please. Agreed?"

Sherry was shocked, but she managed to shake her head yes. Then she turned and looked at Tina who had started talking to her.

"Sherry, we've been roommates for over a year now. During that time we've got really close. You know that several times in the past few months you and I have talked about how worried I am about your drinking and what its been doing to you. We've come close to fighting several times when it came time for us to leave a party That's because I could tell you were drunk and would, consequently, try to get you to let me drive. But you never would let me drive. I can't count the accidents we narrowly escaped . Finally, the other night you got picked up and jailed for a DWI. I worry about you killing yourself or someone else when you're like that and driving."

Tina paused. This wasn't getting any easier, so she'd better plow on through it. It was hard to look at Sherry because she knew how much this must be hurting her.

Then Tina, felt the first tear slide down her cheek, and she reached for a tissue before continuing.

"I'm also worried about these memory lapses you've been having. They always happen when you drink, and we've talked about them possibly being alcoholic blackouts. I also know you're worried about the possibility of being an alcoholic because you grew up with an alcoholic father. I don't want you to have a life like your father's.....that's why I'm here today. I want you to do something to keep that from happening. You've got your entire career ahead of you, and I can't just let you throw it away. Please listen to what people have to say today and decide to get yourself into treatment. I'll do anything I can to help make it easier for you."

Tina was finally done. Mark went next. "Sherry, you and I go back a long way. We've already talked about how you stood me up the other night because you didn't remember having made the date over at my place the other night when we were watching the game. That's because we were drinking at the time...you essentially passed out for hours before you were able to drive home. I'm afraid you may be having blackouts. I'm also worried about your safety if you drink and pass out in public like you did at my place the other night. You're going to be a great nurse, so please do something about this problem before it messes that up for you."

Sherry's hands clenched and unclenched. She reached for a tissue. "Mark, you're not being ...."

Dr. Farwell interrupted her, "Sherry, I asked you to not talk until the others finish. Please be quiet until then, and you'll have your turn."

Sherry sat back in her chair with the tissue clenched in her hand. She looked like she was ready to explode, but she remained quiet.

Sara spoke next. "Sherry, you and I want to the frat party together this last October. You may not remember this, but you fell down the stairs and broke your glasses that night because you were drunk. You just laughed it off. Then you insisted on driving us both home. I was afraid we weren't going to make it home in one piece that night. I've worried about you ever since then, but I've been afraid to say anything. I hope you will decide to get help before this gets worse."

Tom spoke next. "Sherry, you and I were in clinical together last semester, and I smelled alcohol on your breath during report at the start of our shift on two different occasions. You were also late to clinical several times...usually after we'd both been out drinking the night before. I like you Sherry. I don't want to just sit by and watch you do this to yourself."

Sherry reached for another tissue. Somehow she made it through listening to Dr. Terrill explain how if she decided to go into treatment she could makeup the work she missed, and with Christmas break coming up she probably wouldn't miss much school, if any. She also stressed that all of what was said would be kept confidential if she went into the hospital....otherwise all of this information would be given to the school's dean. She also listened to Dr. Brown explain how her insurance benefits covered her getting treatment at two local hospitals. She explained how both were saving a bed for her at this very moment. All she had to do was pick the one she wanted.

Finally, Dr. Farwell turned to her and said. "It's your turn now, Sherry. Please talk to us. We're your friends, we want to listen."

Slowly Sherry got control of herself, and she was finally able to blurt out. "I'm afraid of being an alcoholic. I can't end up like my Dad, I just can't."

Dr. Farwell responded. "No one's calling you an alcoholic Sherry. All we want to do is persuade you to seek treatment for problems related to your drinking. We want you to get help before these problems become even worse. We want you to begin focusing on a solution rather than just trying to ignore them. They won't go away. Let us help you help yourself. Come on, Sherry. Give yourself a chance."

The room was quiet except for the ticking of the clock and the sound of Sherry's crying. Tina moved closer and hugged her. Sherry looked up and saw the concern on her friends' faces before she answered, "OK."

Chapter XVII

FORCED CHOICES

Two nurses sat across from each other at a table in the hospital's cafeteria. They were talking to each other in subdued tones. The youngest of the two was saying. "I don't understand it. Mr. Jones' MAR says he just had something for pain 30 minutes ago. When I answered his call bell, he asked for a pain pill. He swore he hadn't taken anything for pain. Then yesterday morning when I came on duty the night nurse told me she'd only given out two prns for pain on this wing. When you look at the narcotics' records, a definite pattern emerges. It looks as if almost everyone gets something for pain every 3-4 hours on this wing on the evening shift."

Marcy remembered noticing that more pain meds were given on the evening shift before. She'd just assumed it was coincidental. Now she wondered. That's why she'd finally invited her supervisor to coffee so they could talk about it. What had really got her started wondering about all this was their narcotic count had been off several times in the past week. Maybe this wasn't just all coincidence.

Merle found herself listening closely to Marcy. A couple of months ago she would have let it all go in one ear and out the other. Last week she'd attended an administrative workshop where one of the speakers talked about impaired nurses, and now she knew she couldn't ignore what Marcy was saying. Oddly, Marcy was describing some of the characteristics the speaker had listed as being indicators of possible drug addiction. Specifically, a pattern of one shift giving more pain medication than other shifts, narcotic counts being off, and patients reporting little or no relief from pain medication when it was given by a specific nurse. The speaker had lead all of these when he'd read from the manual that the state's peer assistance program for nurses had distributed to hospitals across the state.[1] She'd better investigate this situation further. It sounded pretty serious.

She leaned forward so she could talk softly and still have Marcy hear her. "Marcy, I attended a workshop last week where a man talked about

---

[1] Texas Peer Assistance Program for Nurses Employer Resources Manual: Signs and Symptoms of the Chemically Dependent Nurse, 1990.

impaired nurses. He said to look for patterns when something like this happened. I'm going to ask you some questions he suggested asking when you're trying to determine if a nurse is diverting narcotics. Has there been any one nurse working on these shifts when patients receive more pain meds than usual? Is there someone working this morning that usually works evenings? Is any one nurse involved in the narcotic discrepancies more often than any of the others? Does any one nurse waste more narcotics than any of the other nurses?"[2]

Marcy was frowning as she interrupted Merle, "Whoa, Merle. Slow down. Lets go back to my office and look at the records so I can answer all your questions. I want to be fair."

They both got up from the table and disposed of their empty styrofoam cups in the nearby trash can before they headed out the cafeteria door towards the elevator. Marcy was glad they were by themselves on the elevator as it headed up to the ninth floor so they could continue their conversation.

"You know, Merle, I sure hope we're wrong. I'd hate to have to turn a nurse in for stealing narcotics. It could get really messy."

Merle shook her head. "Yeah. I know what you mean. I think it's a bit easier now than it used to be according to this speaker I heard last week at that workshop. According to him, we don't have to turn a nurse into the board here in Texas anymore unless we want to. Instead, we can call the state's peer assistance program for nurses and report the case. What's more, they'll even provide us with the names of local people who will come help us deal with the nurse. What really surprised me is that if the nurse elects to participate in their peer assistance program, his or her case is never reported to the Board of Nurse Examiners for disciplinary action. The peer assistance program actually allows the nurse to recover from addiction without ever going before the board. Don't get me wrong. They're not easy on the impaired nurse. The peer assistance program monitors the nurse very closely for a two year period. They do all that monitoring to make sure the nurse doesn't relapse."

When they got back to Marcy's office they had the ward clerk bring back the MARs, the staffing schedule, and the narcotic records. It looked like Bill, a nurse who worked for one of the agencies in town and who'd worked for them for a couple of weeks now, was the common denominator in most of what they were investigating. He worked mostly evenings. Most of

[2] Ibid.

the times when the count was off had been times when he was assigned to medications, and he was working this morning. To top it off, Mr. Jones was his patient. He'd also been the nurse most often involved in narcotic wastage. It looked like they had enough of a case to support suspicion of drug impairment, at least enough to support them reporting the case to the state's peer assistance program.

Merle got her notes from the workshop out of her file cabinet so she could be sure that they had covered everything. "Marcy, look at this. I'd forgotten shout this. Here's a list of some other behaviors that can indicate a nurse's functioning is impaired secondary to chemical dependence: being absent from work frequently, being absent for long periods of time while at work, having trouble concentrating, making medication and charting errors, and exhibiting deteriorating job efficiency and rapid mood swings."[3]

Marcy looked thoughtful. She knew Merle would want to know if she'd noted any of these behaviors in Bill.

"I don't think he's absent more than anyone else, but I have noticed that when he is, it's usually at the beginning or end of his days off. We've already talked about it. We know about narcotic charting errors and wastage. The patient saying he doesn't get his pain medication and Bill charting that he's given it; that may be falsifying a patient's record. I've also noticed that he does get angry real fast these days, but it doesn't last long. Mostly he's just real quiet and he stays to himself. He doesn't socialize with any of us. The evening supervisor has complained there are lots of times when she can't find him....that he seems to spend a lot of time in the restroom. Is that what you mean by being absent for long periods of time while at work?"

Merle nodded her head. This matched what she'd heard at the workshop almost perfectly.

"Yes. The workshop speaker called spending excessive amounts of time in the restroom the 'locked door syndrome'.[4] Addicts need the extended privacy to ingest or inject their drug of choice before they go back to work on the units."

* * * * *

---

[3] Hall, L. Employee Assistance Programs: A Key to Early Identification and Treatment. In: Haack, M.R., Hughes, T.L. Addiction in the Nursing Profession. New York: Springer, 1989.

[4] Ibid.

Marcy pulled to a stop at the stoplight. Just her luck to have it turn red. Today had been a long day. She found herself thinking back over everything that had happened. About how supportive the peer assistance program had been when she'd called for help and how Frank, the person they'd had her contact for help locally, had come right over to the hospital to help them review Bill's case. He'd agreed that the nurse was having problems, and he'd spent a lot of time explaining to them what an intervention was. He'd explained it as a session that he and they as representatives of nursing management would have with Bill During this meeting they would confront him in a positive but firm way with documented job performance problems and specified consequent disciplinary action. They would also offer him assistance.[5] In Bill's case, the offer of assistance would take the form of referral to the state's peer assistance program. He'd also stressed that it was important that they focus on job related problems and not get caught up in the trap of diagnosing him as chemically dependent. He'd spent time helping them practice the confrontation, and they'd called Bill in before he left for work and confronted him with the problems they'd noted in his job performance.

The whole ordeal had been very emotionally draining. Merle kept going thinking about all that had happened while she drove. Bill had been extremely defensive and hostile in the beginning. She'd never forget what he'd said when she'd confronted him with the documentation of his falsifying Mr. Jones' MAR by saying he'd given him his pain shot when he hadn't.

He'd yelled at her, "You hysterical bitch. Don't you have anything better to do with your time? Who the hell do you think you are? Just because you're not getting enough at home, you don't have to take your frustrations out on me!"

She was so stunned she couldn't even answer him. Fortunately for her, Frank had interrupted at that point and reminded him that he'd agreed to keep quiet until everyone else had spoken...that he could say whatever he wanted when every one else had talked and it was his turn. Surprisingly, that had kept him quiet until it was his turn to talk.

After both she and Marcy had finished going over their documentation of the performance issues in question, Frank turned to Bill and said, "Bill, these performance issues bother me. They're very serious....regardless of the cause. Falsifying a patient's record is a violation of the nurse practice act. This particular falsification combined with a high incidence of narcotic

---

[5] Ibid.

wastage lends support to the possibility that your performance problems may be related to narcotics. No one is here to accuse you of being an addict, but everyone here is concerned about your performance and your well-being. I want to thank you for staying quiet and listening to what we all had to say. Now, it's your turn to speak."

Bill's eyes shifted hostiley from Frank to Marcy, and to Merle. Then he looked back at Frank.

"Thanks a hell of a lot, man. Nobody's accusing me of being an addict, but you're saying my performance may be affected by narcotics. What a crock. I don't need to put up with this kind of bullshit. You'll be hearing from my lawyer." With that Bill stood up and turned towards the door.

Frank interrupted him before he took the first step. "It's not in your best interest to walk away from this. By law, the falsification of a patient record has to be reported to either the Board of Nurse Examiners or to the state's peer assistance program for nurses. If your case is reported to the Board for investigation you run the risk of facing disciplinary action against your license. The only reason you have the option of having your case handled by the peer assistance program is because the documentation suggests that chemical dependence may be involved. You're lucky in a way because if you choose the peer assistance route, chances are the Board need ever know about this violation."

Bill began to look interested. He slowly sat back down. "What do you mean they might never know? How does this peer assistance stuff work?"

Frank smiled. "First, we go over a lot of legal paper work and make sure you know what you're getting into before you give your voluntary consent to participate. Once we've covered all the information and get all your legal consents, then you voluntarily seek a professional assessment of your chemical dependence status. You also agree to abide by the recommendations specified by the professional who does the assessment. He or she may determine that you have no need for peer assistance for chemical dependence. If that is the case, you can return to work with no further constraints placed on you. On the other hand he or she may decide you need some form of inpatient or outpatient treatment for chemical dependence and ongoing participation in the peer assistance program. If that is the case, you agree to undergo the recommended treatment regimen and to be followed and closely monitored by the peer assistance program for two years. You'll be able to work during that time, but the peer assistance program will closely monitor your job performance. You will have to submit witnessed urine specimens for monthly random drug screens and to attend self-help meetings during the week for the two years that you're a peer assistance participant. If you comply with all the participation stipulations covered in your participation agreement for the two years, you can practice with no further peer assistance stipulations. Both the original complaint and your peer assistance anticipation records remain confidential. Like I said, the Board need never know."

Bill leaned forward in his chair. "You mean my so-called nurse practice violation doesn't get reported to the Board if I participate in the peer assistance program...that participation may simply mean I only have to go through an assessment for chemical dependence and nothing else?"

Frank looked frustrated. "Bill, you're not listening to me. That's one possibility. You have to realize there are lots of other participation stipulations that you may be required to follow. These include treatment, return to work stipulations, meeting attendance, close monitoring, and random drug screens."

Bill continued his questioning. "Yeah, but if I run that risk, I'm not reported to the Board?"

Frank sighed. "Yes, Bill, that's right." Finally Bill had chosen to participate in the peer assistance program. He'd signed the voluntary consents and left with Frank who took him to his assessment appointment.

When she walked into her house she noticed her phone answering machine was blinking. It was a message from Frank. He said that the assessment had supported the need for chemical dependency treatment, and Bill had already signed into a treatment center. The treatment center had agreed to give him a Pro Bono bed for two weeks. Bill's message further explained that it had been a challenge to find a free bed for him, but there was no alternative since Bill worked for an agency and didn't have any insurance benefits.

She called Frank back immediately. She told him how relieved she was that Bill was getting the help he needed. Before she hung up the phone, she made an appointment to meet with Frank at the beginning of next week. They needed to work out a plan for Bill to come to work for them full time after he finished treatment. Frank had already explained that the peer assistance program didn't allow its participants to work for agencies. He promised the peer assistance program would work with them in monitoring Bill's performance for the entire two year period. She and Marcy were sold on the idea, but they needed Frank's help to develop it more fully before they approached administration with the idea.

Merle smiled. Her dog, Taffy, had just jumped in her lap. He hadn't liked sharing her attention with the phone, and now he was making up for lost time. She absent mindedly stroked his head as she spent a few more seconds thinking about all that had happened today. She smiled again as she realized how good it felt to help give a fellow nurse the chance to escape the disease of addiction.

Chapter XVIII

MY WORST ENEMY

Kathy stretched and yawned. She'd been having a really good dream. Its spell had been broken by the sound of the night crew walking down the hallway knocking on doors to wake patients for their vital signs. Waking people at 6:30 AM to take their temperature was obviously for the staff's convenience rather than the patients. She chuckled. This was progress. She was starting to think of herself as a patient rather than a nurse in spite of herself.

God knows, she'd fought it. She couldn't stand to associate with all these addicts when she first got here, but she'd got to be friends with some of them. In fact, after her initial shock had worn off, she'd spent most of her time getting the rest of them to talk about their problems. She'd felt useful, and "playing nurse" like that had kept her mind off her own troubles. At least until they called her on it in group one morning, then she'd had to back off. She'd stayed quiet and uninvolved for several days, but then they'd told her if she continued to stay uninvolved it was like throwing away all the money she'd spent for the insurance that was paying for this treatment.

There was a brisk tap on her door. Before she could respond, Bertha, the night nurse, bustled in with a blood pressure cuff in one hand and an IVAC in the other.

"Good morning, dearie. It's time to rise and shine. The cafeteria will be open for breakfast in about twenty minutes, and then it'll be time for community meeting before you know it. Here, open wide. I need to take your temperature."

It was hard to grimace and hold the IVAC thermometer probe in place, but somehow she managed it. She hated these noxious things. They seemed invasive, somehow, at least the old-time glass thermometers had seemed more personal and user friendly. She also resented Bertha's condescending attitude. She said the same thing to her every morning. It was like she was on automatic pilot and didn't really care about what she was saying or to whom she was saying it. Being called Dearie was like having fingernails scratched down a chalkboard. She'd asked Bertha to call her by her name the first morning they'd met, but her request had fallen on deaf ears.

Kathy got up and took a shower as soon as Bertha finished and left her room. Today was not going to be easy. Her counselor had talked her into allowing a colleague to come visit. Even though Bev was a recovering nurse and had become a counselor after she'd been sober for several years, Kathy doubted that Bev really understood what she was up against.

Bev had been a staff nurse, and being a staff nurse was different from being on faculty. You had to be a role model for your profession when you were faculty. You didn't just have several patients assigned to your care, you had hundreds of students looking up to you. Now that she'd fallen off the proverbial pedestal, admitted her alcoholism and got into treatment, Bev expected her to take things a step further and face her friends from work

When she'd protested, Bev had responded, "Are you willing to go to any lengths to stay in recovery?"

Kathy nodded her head affirmatively, and said, "Yes."

Bev smiled before saying, "Then you need to remember that this is a program of rigorous honesty. You need to face the people in your life, to own your mistakes and to make amends for them if you ever expect to stay in recovery."

So now, here she stood before her mirror, brushing her teeth, and wondering how she could stand letting another faculty member see her in this awkward position of being a patient on a chemical dependence unit. It was hard enough just being on the wrong side of the nurse's station. She was not looking forward to sharing the humiliation with her colleague. Maybe she could catch Bev before the community meeting and talk her into canceling the scheduled visit.

Kathy had just sliced her banana onto her cereal when she saw Bev walk by the cafeteria. She waved at her and motioned at her to come join her. Bev stopped to get a cup of coffee before sitting down at the table across from Kathy She blew the steam off the top of the cup before asking. "How was your night?"

Kathy rolled her eyes. "My night was fine. I've had second thoughts about this meeting with Sheila. I'm not ready to face someone from work. Their attitudes about alcoholism at the university are archaic. Stigma is too nice of a word for what they do to the concept. I need you to call Sheila for me and tell her I can't have visitors."

Bev put down her coffee cup. "Wait a minute. There's something going on here that I think we need to talk about. You are responsible for yourself. Since when did you need me to arrange the details of your personal life? If you've decided to cancel the visit, then you need to be assertive and take responsibility for canceling it yourself. That means you'll also need to face the consequences of your actions. It sounds like you're afraid to face Sheila----either in person or on the phone. What's going on?"

Kathy glanced furtively around the cafeteria. Thankfully, it was empty except for she and Bev.

"I don't know. I guess I'm just afraid of what she'll think of me. I don't want to be a failure in her eyes. I don't want her going back and telling everyone on the faculty that I'm just another alcoholic that's fallen by the wayside."

To her amazement, Bev actually chuckled. Kathy felt herself getting angry. Her voice shook as she glared at Bev and said.

"I'm glad you find this amusing. Here I am spilling my guts out to you and you laugh. Some counselor you are ... to say nothing of the kind of nurse you are. What kind of nurse would laugh at a patient at a time like this?"

Bev chuckled again. "A good one, that's what kind. Listen to yourself. You've taken up residence on the pity pot, and you've lost the ability to look at this objectively. What's this 'just another alcoholic fallen by the wayside bullshit'? Alcoholism is a disease. There is no place for moralistic blaming and judgment when you're dealing with a disease. You know that; you're a nurse."

Kathy tried to interrupt, but Bev put out her hand and motioned for Kathy to stop before continuing. "Wait a minute, let me finish here. Some where along the line most of us who are nurses begin to believe that because our business is helping sick people help themselves, we can't be sick ourselves. We begin to think we are immune to diseases and other human frailties. We see ourselves as above humanity, condescendingly stooping from time to time to self-righteously administer to their needs. Or worse, we expect ourselves to be perfect and always take care of others before we take care of ourselves. We become our own worst enemy. Our own attitudes and prejudices turn on us; we can't accept our humanity or our disease. So we drink more. We do more drugs. We compulsively overeat. We get involved in unhealthy, co-dependent relationships. We lose ourselves in the morass of our unrealistic self-expectations, false pride and denial. Then when we hit bottom and are forced to do something about healing ourselves. Only our attitudes and self-blame keep putting up obstacles. Instead of 'Physician, heal thyself' we need to focus instead on the phrase, 'Nurse, heal thyself'. If we can't love ourselves enough to do that, then all the love and efforts we make to heal others is nothing but a false facade we put up so we can keep hiding from ourselves."

Kathy was speechless. Bev had never talked like this before. Bev must have seen the surprise in her expression. Her tone softened before she continued.

"Kathy, I'm sorry. I got reminded of some of my own issues as a recovering nurse and took them out on you. I was my own worst enemy for a long time. Sometimes I see the traits I didn't like in myself in others. All I can ask you to do is to think about what I've just said. Treat it like a meeting....take what you like and leave the rest. That means decide what parts of it, if any, apply to you, act accordingly, and ignore the rest."

Kathy nodded. "OK. I wondered why you got so intense all of a sudden. You may be right. You've certainly given me lots to think about."

Bev smiled. "We've got to run or we'll be late for community meeting. Think about what we've talked about, and when we have our session this morning you can let me know what you've decided to do about Sheila's visit."

Kathy was already up and on the way to depositing her tray as she responded. "Sure. Will do."

Kathy was so busy thinking about what Bev had said during the meeting that she hardly paid any attention to the meeting itself. Maybe Bev was right. Maybe she did have a sort of reverse ego problem. Maybe always putting others and their needs before herself wasn't as selfless and Christ-like as she'd like to think. Maybe it was a way of denying her own problems and avoiding taking care of her own issues. Maybe being a nurse was her way of trying to buy some self-validation and self-respect. Maybe she did need to help others to feel good about herself. Maybe she'd put herself on a damn pedestal. And maybe she was the punitive judge that kept condemning herself over and over again for falling off the pedestal and sentencing herself to continued self-blame.

She wished she'd never waved at Bev this morning. She'd certainly opened quite a can of worms. Suddenly, her eyes wandered to the twelve steps hanging on the dayroom wall. This time when she read, "We admitted we were powerless over alcohol --- that our lives had become unmanageable"[1] she saw the part about her life becoming unmanageable for the first time.

---

[1] Alcoholics Anonymous (1976). Alcoholics Anonymous. Third Edition, Alcoholics Anonymous: New York, p. 59.

All of a sudden she knew that this whole recovery thing wasn't just about her alcoholism anymore. It was about her life. It was about facing her humanity. She had to give herself permission to be human and to accept the reality of being unable to manage her life before she could start healing herself. Bev had said that only a higher power could manage lives. She'd also said the second step was about accepting that only a higher power could manage our lives and that the third step was about actually letting a higher power manage our lives. She knew she was on to something, so she quickly read the second and third steps. The second was: "Came to believe that a Power greater than ourselves could restore us to sanity".[2] The third was "Made a decision to turn our will and our lives over to the care of God as *we understood Him*".[3] It suddenly dawned on her that these words weren't just about drinking. They were about her life. How she lived. How she thought. How she acted.

Suddenly she realized the room had got quiet and everyone was looking at her. Someone must have asked her a question. She stammered. "I'm sorry. I was thinking about something."

Bev smiled. "Whatever it was, it must have been pretty heavy duty. We've been waiting for you to tell us your goal for the day. Instead, why don't you share with the group what had you lost in such deep thought?"

Always before in group Kathy had spent most of her time listening or redirecting the group's attention to another patient. She'd always found herself asking another patient what they thought or felt. This time was going to bc different.

"Well, I'm not sure this is going to make any sense. I've been here not almost a week and I've spent most of thc time 'playing nurse' and focusing on others rather than myself. Today I'm beginning to realize that that's my way of escaping from facing myself and owning by disease. When you caught me deep in thought, I was involved in really reading the first three steps for the first time."

She took a deep breath before continuing. "I just figured out that they're about more than my drinking. They're about living. They're about recovery. They're about being human instead of playing God. I've used being a nurse to keep from facing myself. I'd convinced myself that if I were a good enough nurse then I must be an okay person. I kept paying the price of expecting myself to be perfect and more than human. Of course I always

[2] Ibid.

[3] Ibid.

failed. And I drank rather than feel the pain of failure and disappointment. All these years I fooled myself into thinking that I accepted alcoholism as a disease. The truth was that I really saw it as symptomatic of moral failure. Otherwise, it wouldn't have taken me so long to see it in myself."

She paused, then continued. "Today I'm expecting a visit from another nurse who's on the nursing school faculty with me. I'd convinced myself not to see her because I'd decided she'd judge me as a moral failure. I thought she'd see me as 'just another alcoholic fallen by the wayside'. Bev helped me see that I was projecting my own negative judgmental attitudes on to someone else. Really reading these steps this morning has helped me see that its OK to be powerless, its OK to have an 'unmanageable life'---that's part of being human. And so is being an alcoholic. So my goal for today is to start letting myself be human so I can love myself as I am rather than only loving myself when I meet self-imposed unrealistic expectations."

The room was quiet. Too quiet. Maybe she'd said too much, self-disclosed too much. Then Bev started clapping. The whole room started applauding and cheering her. Finally everyone was quiet. Then Bev quietly said. "Welcome to the human race." After they closed the group the usual way with the Lord's Prayer, everyone hugged her and thanked her for sharing what she'd been thinking with the group.

* * * * *

Later that evening, Kathy and Sheila were sitting on a bench outside on the hospital grounds. The were watching the fountain spray its plumes of water into the spring-tinged air. Kathy remembered back to when she'd first walked out to the lounge to greet Sheila. The first thing Sheila had done was to hug Kathy. The first thing she'd said was, "Kathy it must have been so hard for you to do this. It took such courage. I really admire you for having the strength to do what you've done. I want to do whatever I can to support you through your treatment and on into your recovery."

Kathy had laughed before saying, "You don't know how good it feels to hear that. I'm laughing because yesterday I spent lots of time worrying about this visit. I imagined that you'd be critical of me and tell everyone at work what a sick alcoholic failure I was. This morning I finally realized that it was my own attitude that was the problem. Having you offer your empathy and support like this really shows me that I have been my own worst enemy for a long time. Thank you for coming and for being such a good friend."

They had enjoyed a good visit after that, and they'd ended up outside here by the fountain. When Sheila got up to leave, Kathy was surprised to realize she actually hated to see Sheila go. She realized that she'd never really let her friends give her any support before. Maybe allowing herself to be human wasn't going to be so bad after all.

Chapter XIX

WHO DO YOU THINK YOU ARE

Pam braked sharply to avoid the driver in front of her who suddenly decided to turn left. She swore nobody in this entire state knew how to use a turn signal. Her irritation was momentary, and in a few seconds she started thinking again about what a headache today was going to be at work. It had only been a few days since she, her peer assistance advocate and her head nurse had a return to work conference. She still remembered how tense that conference had been for her. It had felt like she was giving away control of her professional life forever. She wanted to get up and walk out, but she couldn't. If she had, she'd have been walking out on her career as a nurse. She couldn't afford that.

If she went along with the dictates of the peer assistance program, then she could continue to practice nursing. Then the state board of nursing would never be told about the violations of the Nurse Practice Act she'd committed because of her addiction to Demerol. She'd signed a participation agreement that required her to work according to the stipulations of the peer assistance program for one year. She'd have to live under the same stipulations in her private life (drug/alcohol free and attending four self-help meetings a week) for a total of two years from the date she signed the agreement. Right now the two years seemed like an eternity, and she was worried that the year's time on the job just might be unbearable.

The return to work stipulations of the agreement were pretty stiff. She couldn't give narcotics for six months, she couldn't float to other units or work over-time or off-shifts. She couldn't work for agencies and she had to meet with her immediate supervisor once a week. She had to work full time for an entire year----and the worst of it was, she had to have random drug screens done every month for the entire two years whether she was working or not! Big brother really was watching, and she'd better march to his drum or she'd be facing a disciplinary hearing before the state board.

She was almost to work, and she still didn't know what she was going to tell her co-workers. How was she going to explain why she couldn't give narcotics or even have access to them? Her peer assistance advocate said that she could trade off duties with them...do a bunch of treatments for them so they could do medications for her. That all sounded well and good in theory. But she could just hear the laughter---or worse, see the hostile glares---that she'd be on the receiving end of the first time she told her co-workers that that she couldn't give medications. They'd either hate her for getting "special treatment" or they'd immediately know she was a recovering drug addict. That meant she'd be branded in the professional community from then on and reacted to accordingly.

Her Narcotics' Anonymous sponsor told her that she had to do what it takes to get clean and stay clean. That a drug free existence was the most important thing in her life and that she'd embarked on a "program of rigorous honesty". When she'd tried to tell her sponsor what would happen when she was honest about her problem at work, her sponsor had merely smiled. Then she'd said, "There are no big deals, Pam. You have to decide what's most important to you---your life or your ego and false pride."

That had hurt. The words had stuck with her, and she had to admit that her sponsor was right. When it came to deciding between dying or living with a blow to your pride, embarrassment and shame seemed more acceptable.

A few minutes later, Pam found herself in report. When assignments were made it became obvious that she wasn't being assigned medications. Instead she was doing treatments and her LPN was doing all the medications. She felt people looking at her, and she knew she had to say something. She might as well try this honesty bit her sponsor kept pushing on her.

She took a deep breath before speaking. "I'm sure you noticed that I won't be giving medications. I need to be honest with you if I'm going to work with you as part of a team. Most of you have worked with me before, so you know I'm a hardworking team member. We've all supported each other for a long time. Most of you know I've been away from work on extended sick leave. What I'm going to tell you now is one of the hardest things I've ever done."

All eyes were on her. She took a swallow of coffee before continuing. "I know the peer assistance people have been here before during in-services. We've all heard that drug addiction and alcoholism are diseases and not a sign of weak will power or bad morals. Its hard to look at it that way when it affects someone you know personally. Therefore, I'm asking everyone in this room to keep what I'm going to tell you confidential."

She looked around the report room, and she saw heads nodding. So far so good. Here goes, she'd come too far now not to take the plunge.

"The reason I can't give medications is because I'm a recovering Demerol addict. I've been in treatment for my addiction and its been over a month since I've used any drugs or alcohol. I'm a participant in the peer assistance program. One of their requirements is that I not give---or have access to narcotics of other mood altering medications for the first six months that I'm back to work. They also suggested I tell all of you what I'm going through and have my advocate come in and do an in-service on addictions with an emphasis on how to prevent relapse and spot relapse when it happens..."

Brad interrupted her, "What's relapse?"

What a relief. She'd thought he was going to tell her how shocked and disappointed he was in her. Instead, he just needed her to explain what relapse was. In her hurry to get this over , she forgot she hadn't known what relapses were until she'd learned about them in treatment.

"Thanks, Brad. Relapse is when someone starts using again. You all need to know about that so you can recognize when I'm having a bad time and get me the help I need before I start using again .... or, God forbid, know how to recognize behaviors in me that would mean I'd probably started using again. The peer assistance program believes I have a better chance of staying clean and in recovery if my co-workers know what indicates relapse. That way they can help me keep from starting to use again. They're right. Once you know how to recognize whether I'm using again or not, its going to be a lot harder for me to slip back into my disease because I won't be able to hide it from you like I did before."

The room was quiet. She'd expected lots of anger and blaming. She'd never imagined that they'd just sit there looking shocked. What should she do now? Then she remembered the step about making amends to those she'd harmed because of her addiction. She had a lot of ground to cover in that department, but maybe this was a good place to start.

She took another sip of her coffee. "I can tell by your reaction that you're pretty upset. I realize I've really let you down. I've disappointed you. It'll take me a long time to win back your trust. I may never win it back, but I want to say I am sorry for hurting you. I also want to ask you to try to find room in your hearts to forgive me. I want to be a real member of this team again. I'm not special or fragile. It is okay for you to criticize me and confront me. Honest communication will be important; so, I want you to be as honest with me as I am going to be with you. I know that's asking you to believe a lot since I was dishonest for so long about my using. I know I'm talking too much. We've got patients out there to take care of, so let me just say, I'm sorry."

There, she'd said it. Now it was up to them. A few smiled at her as they all walked out of report. During the morning and throughout the day all but one of her co-workers took her aside and told her they admired her courage in being as honest as she had been. They offered to help support her recovery in any way they could. A couple had adamantly insisted that she didn't need to apologize or ask for their forgiveness because what she'd done had been part of her illness. They said if she'd imagine being a diabetic instead of an addict, she'd see how ridiculous it was to apologize. She'd been brutally honest with them in response to that suggestion. She'd told them diabetics didn't lie or steal or shoot up or use patients medications. They'd told her every diabetic they sneaked '"forbidden foods" and cheated on their diets.

"Who knows" , they'd added, "if they had a chance, they probably helped themselves to tempting desserts and snacks from used patients' food trays."

* * * * *

A few weeks later they had a patient code. She and Brad responded about the same time, everyone else was already there. Brad handed her the clipboard so she could document everything, and he took over handling the code's medication. After the code was over, they both headed for the staff lounge. They knew from years of working together that they needed to sit down immediately after a code and process what had happened. Otherwise, the feelings and emotions became so bad that you started to turn them off and then you were headed towards big time burnout.

Brad was sitting with his head down. He absent mindedly rubbed his temples with his right hand. Pan wanted to smoke a cigarette, but knew she'd have to wait until she could get away for a break and go outside. Without thinking, she sat down next to Brad and started massaging the back of his neck. She found herself softly asking, "It was pretty rough in there wasn't it?" Brad nodded, and she continued, "You did a good job with the meds. I'm sorry that I couldn't do the meds for us. As soon as I can I'll do all of the code meds for a long time to make up for it."

Brad was quiet, but then he slowly spoke. "You don't need to do that Pam. I've seen you working around here, you do your share and more. Like you always did. You're still a super nurse, and I'd rather work with you than anyone else. I know I've been avoiding you, but I had to have time to think. It helped when that lady came and did the in-service and explained the disease process of addictions and how recovery works. I have to admit, the more I see of the new you, the more I like you. I'm beginning to think my anger and mistrust in the beginning was probably out of line."

She smiled, then she said, "No, it wasn't. You trusted me both as a friend and a co-worker. I betrayed that trust. When things began to go wrong for me, I intentionally kept it from you. And I did things a nurse should never do. You'd had me on this 'super nurse' pedestal, and I fell off big time. It's pretty natural to me that it'll take a while for me to earn back some of that trust. I'm just grateful that you are giving me a chance to do so. I've missed you. This is the first time we've really talked since I came back to work, and I can't tell you how good it feels. There is one thing, I'd really appreciate it if you stopped thinking of me as a 'super nurse'....I don't want back on any pedestals. I'm painfully aware right now of just how human and capable of mistakes I am professionally or personally."

Brad stuck out his hand, "Let's make a deal", he said. "I'll not be putting you on any pedestals if you quit putting yourself down for what you did before you went into treatment."

Pam smiled as she shook hands. "Brad," she said, "you've got a deal."

* * * * *

Several months later Pam was working on a weekend. The other nurse called in sick. That meant she was working with an agency nurse. Things went pretty smoothly until one of Pam's patients needed a pain injection and she had to ask the other nurse to give it. The other woman practically sneered.

"What's wrong with you? You think you're too good to give a shot once in a while? I've carried my load around here, what I want to know is why don't you carry yours. Where do you get off asking me to do your work?"

Pam felt her facial muscles tense up. Well, she thought, here it is. This is the big confrontation I was so afraid of when I first came back to work. I have to say something. Well here goes.

"I realize I'm asking a lot. You're right, you've been very good about doing your share of the work. You don't know that I'm under a peer assistance agreement with the state's peer assistance program and I can't give narcotics for another month. What I can do is offer to do some of your other duties in return for you covering my narcotics."

The woman's mouth fell open. Then she put her hands on both hips and looked down her nose at Pam.

"You mean to stand there and tell me you're one of them 'drug addicts'? You shouldn't even be working. I have half a mind to turn you into the state board myself. The very idea....a drug addict working as a nurse. I never in my wildest dreams thought I'd see the day when I had to work with an addict."

Then she turned her pack on Pam. "I'm going to lunch. You can bloody well do what you want with the med keys!"

With this, she turned and flung the keys down on the nurses' station a few feet from where Pam was sitting.

For a few seconds, Pam just sat there replaying in her mind what had just happened. What should she do? Then she knew. She reached for the phone and called the nursing supervisor. She told her what had happened, and the supervisor said she'd be right there. While she waited, Pam kept an eye on the medication keys. She asked the ward clerk to watch them too because she wanted to make sure she had a witness that she didn't touch them. When the supervisor got there, she picked up the keys and gave Pam's patient the pain injection. Then she asked Pam to talk with her in the head nurse's office that was just off the nurse's station for a minute.

The supervisor interviewed Pam about what happened and wrote the specific details in an anecdotal note. She did the same thing with the ward clerk who had witnessed the exchange between Pam and the agency nurse. Then she'd told them to go back to work and had said she'd be back later to talk to the agency nurse. Later that afternoon, just before change of shift report, the supervisor returned. She called both the agency nurse and Pam into the head nurse's office. She confronted the agency nurse with the inappropriateness of her behavior. She stressed how unprofessional it had been to say what she had in a relatively public setting where patients and their visitors could hear. She also pointed out that it was very unprofessional to leave the narcotic keys lying out where anyone could pick them up, and how inappropriate it was to refuse to cooperate. She told the agency nurse if she failed to keep Pam's recovery status confidential she could be sued for libel. She told the nurse that she'd spoken with the agency's administrator, and that she was sending him a copy of the documentation of this disciplinary counseling. She ended by saying that after today, the hospital would not allow her to work for them again. The agency nurse remained angry and defensive. She never apologized for any of her actions.

* * * * *

That night after her Narcotics Anonymous meeting, Pam called her sponsor. She needed to process with her what had happened during the day. First, she'd talked about what happened in the meeting when the group's leader had asked if anyone had anything they needed to talk about. The meeting had turned into a discussion of how the various participants handled resentment. What they'd said helped. Talking to her sponsor helped too. Her sponsor told her to read the "Freedom from Bondage" story in the Big Book and to pay close attention to the directions for dealing with resentment at the end of the chapter. Specifically, she told Pam to pray for the agency nurse every day for a minimum of two weeks and to pray for that nurse to receive everything Pam wanted for herself. Her sponsor told her that at first it would feel gimmicky---but that she should continue to do it anyway and to "act as if". Her sponsor promised that eventually she'd stop resenting the agency nurse and that all her anger and hurt would slip away.

Her sponsor also stressed that harboring resentments and anger only hurts ourselves because it takes tremendous energy to keep it fueled...instead she could use the energy in healthy, positive ways that would benefit Pam rather than harming her. Pam had to agree, she knew the toll prolonged stress took on the human body. She'd learned about that in nursing school, and she'd certainly seen what it did to her patients. Her sponsor also talked about an Alcoholic's Anonymous concept called "healthy detachment". According to her sponsor that meant being careful not to own responsibility for the negativity we encounter in our lives, that it meant letting go of something and realizing that it was the other person's problem and not her own. She'd ended by saying, "Pam, you need to use the resentment prayer, and you need to work on telling yourself that the agency nurse's attitude was her problem....and not yours. You'll need to make yourself repeat that in your mind every time you find yourself thinking about what the agency nurse said to you. It's late now, so I'm going to say good-bye. I want you to figure out what you want for yourself and to use that in saying the resentment prayer. Then I want you to get some sleep."

Pam thanked her and said good-bye.

Surprisingly, the hardest part of following her sponsor's assignment was figuring out what she really wanted for herself. She remembered a Lakota friend of hers. He had talked to her about prayer and his tribe's belief that it was always important to ask for "health and happiness for all the people". She could start with that prayer. She knew she wanted that for herself and that working her twelve step program was helping her find it.

Chapter XX

CHASING BUTTERFLIES

Kim closed the kardex. She'd just finished giving change of shift report and she couldn't wait to get home and get out of her uniform. Kyle was coming over tonight, and she was looking forward to spending some time with him. She usually went to a meeting on Friday nights, but this was a special occasion. It was Kyle's birthday. She hoped he'd enjoy the romantic dinner for two she had planned for his birthday. What a relief to have an excuse to miss tonight's AA meeting. She'd been finding the meetings a real bore lately anyway.

She'd called the Peer Assistance office to report that she wouldn't be going to the meeting because she had been having diarrhea all day. She knew that she was lying, but it was such a harmless lie. Besides, sharing Kyle's birthday with him was worth a little white lie.

She'd be done with the peer assistance program in another two weeks. Thank God, then she wouldn't have to go to four meetings every week and get someone to sign her attendance documentation form. She'd understood going to meetings was important in supporting her sobriety in the beginning. She'd gone to meetings and stayed sober almost two years now, and she hated hearing the same old stuff week in and week out. Her sponsor kept telling her meetings would always be an essential part of staying sober, but Kim knew plenty of folks who only went to meetings now and then.

The evening charge nurse was waiting for her to make rounds with him. Kim forced herself to stop thinking about the evening ahead while she completed the rounds with him. Then she headed for the elevators, traveled down five floors, went out the front door and headed across the parking lot to her car.

On the way home she kept thinking about how Kyle had wanted to go dancing this evening. Maybe they'd slip out for some dancing at a local club after they'd finished their dinner. They'd been going to a local club once or twice a month to dance. At first he had seemed uncomfortable because she didn't drink. Now he took it as a matter of course and no longer tried to convince her to drink with him. He seemed to understand that she couldn't drink because she used to have problems when she drank.

With just two weeks left of her required peer assistance participation, she was really looking forward to having more evenings free to spend with Kyle. Things had just been going too well lately. She was used to her life being full of adventure and chaos. Seems like she'd always been in trouble one way or another in the past, and all her previous boyfriends had been real losers. Things were not that way now, and she found herself being almost bored. All of this success was frightening, but not as frightening as having a relationship with a man who treated her decently and said he loved her. She had a feeling Kyle was thinking about asking her to marry him, and she got uncomfortable just thinking about what she'd do if that happened.

She'd grown up in an alcoholic home, so this was her first encounter with what society labeled "normal". Her sponsor kept telling her that she'd get used to it. She'd explained that serenity and peace of mind resulted from working the twelve steps. She'd said that addicts and alcoholics who grew up in dysfunctional families and had always been involved in dysfunctional lifestyles and relationships often found the program's gifts of serenity and peace of mind boring when they first experienced them. Kim remembered her sponsor had warned her that feeling this particular type of boredom was often a red flag that warned of pending relapse. She'd just looked at her sponsor and laughed before saying.

"Being bored because you feel peaceful and serene causing someone to start drinking again? That's crazy!"

She was almost home now. Two more lights and she could turn off onto her road. With this traffic, it might take a while before she got there. Sure, she was bored with all this recovery crap, but that didn't mean she was ready to drink again. That would mean throwing away these past two years of hard work. With her luck, it would also mean getting reported to the Board of Nurse Examiners and ending up on probation. The least that would happen if she got caught drinking again is that she'd have to spend two more years participating in peer assistance. No, thank you.

Later that night Kim was barely aware of the traffic sounds in the background or of the beer can she stepped over as she walked through the parking lot to the club's entrance. She was still fuming over getting stood up for dinner. She'd got home, fixed the dinner, had the table set, the candles lit, and the music playing. It was the perfect setting for a romantic evening. Only Kyle never showed up. Finally, about 9:00 PM he'd called. He'd sounded drunk. He'd been very apologetic. The guys from work had talked him into going to the club after work to celebrate his birthday, and they'd been celebrating ever since. It wasn't until someone mentioned grabbing a bite to eat for supper that he realized he'd forgotten their dinner date. He apologized profusely and invited her to join them. So, here she was.

Waves of smoke and loud music swept over her as she entered the crowd after being carded at the door. She paused to glance at the dance floor. There was Kyle, but he wasn't alone. He was dancing with a gorgeous redhead, and they seemed oblivious to the world abound them. Kim was frozen to the spot. She couldn't believe what she was seeing. Then she started in on herself for being such a fool. She should have known Kyle was going to be just like the rest of the men in her life had been....it had just been a matter of time. Funny, this time the "honeymoon" had lasted longer. Maybe she was just getting more gullible.

What was only a few minutes seemed like a few hours, but finally the song was over and Kyle and the redhead broke apart. Kim recognized some of the men at the table they were walking towards. Kyle had introduced her to them at his office Christmas party. One of them must have noticed her. He leaned towards Kyle and said something to Kyle. Kyle turned and looked for her and then motioned for her to come join them.

Kyle was smiling as she approached. "Hi, Kim. I'm so glad you came. You know Pete and Mike from work. This is George, and that's Mario."

Then he turned to the woman with whom he'd been dancing before saying, "And this is April. The boys had her fly in from Omaha this evening to help me celebrate my birthday. We used to be neighbors. The boys had heard me talk about her and all the things we used to do together, so they thought they'd surprise
me."

She forced herself to smile and extend her hand. "Hi, April. Welcome to San Antonio. How was your flight?"

April shook her hand as she replied, "Oh, not bad. I almost think the layover in Dallas took longer than the flight."

Kim replied, "I know what you mean. How long are you going to be staying?"

April sighed, "I'm afraid only a few days. I have to get back to the office for a board meeting next Tuesday."

Kim sat down and ordered a Virgin Mary. The waitress must have been new because Kim had to explain that was the same as a Bloody Mary only without the alcohol. She'd only taken a few sips of her drink when George asked her to dance. As soon as they got up, Kyle and April got up too and the four of them headed for the dance floor. Kim couldn't help noticing how comfortable they were with each other, and she was beginning to resent it.

She smiled and looked up at George, "Tell me about April. She seems like a nice person." George answered, "I don't know that much about her. I just know Kyle talks about Omaha and April a lot. They must have been more than neighbors. You can see it in the way his eyes light up when he talks about her. I thought you knew about April. However, judging from the look on your face when you first spotted her tonight, I'd say he hadn't told you about her. Am I right?"

Kim rolled her eyes. "How perceptive of you, George. Did you guys plan this just to make my day, or what?"

George chuckled. "Of course not. I'm glad you know. I think its only fair. Besides, now I can have an excuse to spend some time with you."

Kim looked puzzled as she said. "Why , George. Are you flirting with me?"

A big smile spread over George's face. "Why, yes. I guess you could say that. And you want to know what else I think? I think you should take advantage of it and do everything in your power to make Kyle jealous. Let's give him a run
for his money. Who knows, maybe you and I can salvage something out of tonight after all. Why don't you start by letting me buy you a real drink. Then you and I will be on our way to being the life of the party."

Kim had to think about that one. It was tempting. She knew if she had a drink she'd be able to endure this evening a lot better. She felt hurt and abandoned. Even though George's attention helped a little bit, a drink would help a whole lot more. Besides, she knew if she drank in front of Kyle, maybe he'd realize how much she was hurting. Maybe he'd realize it was because he'd stood her up earlier and because he'd never mentioned already being involved with another woman. She wanted him to feel responsible for wrecking her sobriety.

Suddenly Kim smiled. This must be what the old timers at the meetings referred to as "stinking thinking". They were right. Any more thoughts like that, and she'd be throwing almost two years down the drain. Maybe there was a way to make him feel guilty without having to ruin her sobriety.

"George, honey. I'm driving so I don't want to get drunk. But you're right, a drink would taste mighty good about now. Why don't you get me one of those new non-alcoholic beers? At least then I can have the taste of getting drunk without getting drunk or having a hangover."

The music stopped. "Sure thing, little lady. I'll go get that fake beer for you right now and meet you back at the table."

As Kim walked back to the table she decided that she was going to show Kyle a thing or two....he was going to think she started drinking and smoking again and that she didn't give a damn about him or his little Miss Omaha.

She sat down and turned to Mario. "Mario, would you mind if I had one of your cigarettes?"

"No, of course not. Here, help yourself."

Kim took the cigarette and placed it between her lips. As Mario leaned in to light it for her, she let her hand linger on his. It had been a long time, but she still remembered how sensuous sharing the lighting of a cigarette this way could be. Mere touch sometimes spoke volumes. She hoped Kayle noticed. Out of the corner of her eye she saw him watching. Maybe this would work. He started to say something to her, but before he could get anything out, George was back with her drink.

"Here you go little lady. Just for you. Drink up."

This time Kyle really did a double take. She loved it. He was noticing her. She'd show him. She turned to George and kissed him on the cheek.

"Why thank you, George. You're so sweet. I didn't get a chance to tell you earlier....you're a great dancer!"

George beamed. "You're not so bad yourself, little lady."

Without thinking Kim automatically took a sip of her drink. She was surprised it tasted so much like beer. Her sponsor had warned her not to drink the fake beers. She'd said they had a tiny amount of alcohol in them and that the taste could trigger a relapse. How ridiculous.

After that, Kim got caught up in the whirl of party. She actually enjoyed showing Kyle what fun she could have with his buddies. He spent most of him time dancing with April, but she did catch him looking at her and frowning several times during the evening. That wasn't enough. She wanted to be in his arms and have April be the one focusing her attention on his buddies. This evening just wasn't going the way she'd planned it.

Her life was never going to change. She was always going to be a loser. At least she was used to that; it was familiar territory. These past 23 months in the peer assistance program had been a joke. It was scary trying to stay sober and to "be normal". Look where it got her. Just then the slow dance she and George were dancing ended. She glanced across the dance floor just in time to see Kyle embrace April and kiss her.

That did it, she'd really show him. "George, honey. Could you get me a double scotch on the rocks? I've decided I'd like to let you drive me home so I don't have to worry about not getting drunk anymore."

George laughed. "It's about time you came to your senses. I know seeing Kyle with April must be eating you alive. I'll be right back, and there will be more where that one came from. I'll take care of you tonight."

The rest of the night was a blur. She remembered drinking and dancing and necking with George out on the dance floor. She remembered Kyle trying to talk her into stopping drinking and offering to take her home. She'd just laughed at him and told him he was just jealous because she was getting along so well with George. She'd eventually left with George.

* * * * *

A week had passed since that night. She and George had tied one on and drank the entire weekend away. She'd evidently had a blackout because she didn't remember a lot of what her counselor told her had happened. Evidently, she'd not shown up for work, and her supervisor had called her. She'd must have sounded really drunk on the phone. Then, when she showed up for work Tuesday, she'd had several drinks before she went to work. Of course, they demanded that she let them do a stat drug and alcohol screen. They had the right to make such a demand because of her peer assistance agreement. To make a long story short, the test results were positive for alcohol. They'd sent her home and reported her to the peer assistance program.

The next thing she knew, she was given the choice of going back into treatment and starting her peer assistance participation over or being turned over to the Board of Nursing for disciplinary action. She'd asked to call her sponsor so she could help her decide. Telling her sponsor what had happened hadn't been easy. Her sponsor had told her to agree to the treatment and peer assistance participation. Her sponsor had also volunteered to come drive her to the treatment center.

On the way to the treatment center, Kim started talking about having to re-start her peer assistance participation.

"Mary, I just can't stand the thought of having to do all this for two more years. It was bad enough having to comply with all that structure and rules and crap these past 23 months. Now I'm facing two weeks in treatment and another 23 months and two weeks in the peer assistance program. I know I need to detox. But I don't need to repeat the two years in peer assistance."

Suddenly, Mary pulled off the road and slammed on the brakes. She looked furious as she turned to Kim. Kim had never heard her sound so stern.

"Kim, what you don't seem to realize is that you have a choice here. We aren't talking about a temporary two year reprieve from drinking and drugging here. We're talking about the rest of your life. You can choose life or death. If you choose death by drinking, it can be a slow and painful death. Or it can be fast and harmful to others if you die in a car accident you've caused. Either way, choosing to immerse yourself in the disease hurts others as well as yourself. You've got to get your priorities straight. Your life is worth two years of complying with peer assistance monitoring. You're worth it. You can't afford to let success scare you this time. You can't keep returning to the disease just because its familiar and you know what to expect. That's like walking out in front of a speeding train because you can see it and you know what to expect. Life is a gift and you need to love yourself enough to give yourself permission to enjoy it."

Kim just looked at her. What Mary was saying hit home. Mary continued, only this time in a softer tone.

"If you can picture your two alternatives as vivid images, well then, maybe that'll make it easier to choose life over death. When you think of taking a drink or using a drug, think of standing in front of a speeding train. Think of soaring high and free as a butterfly when you think of living sober. A butterfly symbolizes a beginning, a starting over. Now we can be sober. Just like the butterfly has to follow certain laws of physics to fly, we have to follow the 12 steps and the AA program to stay sober."

Mary took a deep breath before continuing. "You will have to stay sober one day at a time for the rest of your life ---- not just for the months you spend in the peer assistance program. So yes, you need to detox. You also need the rest of your life lived sober, one day at a time. Just like the butterfly needed to learn to fly, we need to learn to live sober. And the AA program shows us how. Stopping drinking is the easy part, it's living sober that's the real kicker."

She reached into the back seat of her car and got her copy of the Big Book. "Here, there's something I want you to read while you're in treatment. It's the chapter entitled "A.A. Taught him to Handle Sobriety".[1]

Then she'd let me out at the front door. The last thing she said to me was: "You have to take the first step of the rest of your life yourself."

I keep thinking of all the times in meetings when people talked about being "happy, joyous and free" because of working the AA program. Maybe Mary was right. I'm going to have to keep my mind focused on being that butterfly.

---

[1] Alcoholics Anonymous (1979). Alcoholics Anonymous Third Edition, New York: Alcoholics Anonymous World Services, Inc.

EPILOGUE

EPILOGUE

The collection of short stories in this book were designed to experientially guide readers through the complicated worlds of chemical dependency, its treatment, and the application of twelve-step group philosophy and principles to the promotion of recovery. Their content illustrated how chemical dependence is an equal opportunity disease and how, although its experience is similar, it experience is also unique for a wide variety of individuals --- be they students, nurses, grandmothers, adolescents or homosexuals.

Specifically, this book used story telling to covertly teach the reader about interventions, blackouts, withdrawals, Antabuse therapy, group techniques, defusing staff conflicts, assorted biases, peer assistance, and recovery. Furthermore, this book depicted how difficult recovery can be and how important it is to work with a sponsor and to stay involved in twelve-step programs. Hopefully, it clarified that relapse does not have to be the end of the world, but can instead serve as an important step towards recovery.

In closing, the intent of the short stories in this book was to take its readers on a flight of fancy that jarred and perhaps changed attitudes so that the reader might be more empathetic the next time they see a "butterfly struggling to fly." Along the way, it is hoped that the reader also learned about the magic of chemical dependency nursing. And finally, it is hoped that these stories will have planted seeds of hope where they are most needed so that more may enjoy the freedom of recovery.